C000254644

AQA GCSE
Media Studies
Revision Guide

Steff Hutchinson

Published in 2019 by Illuminate Publishing Ltd, PO Box 1160,
Cheltenham, Gloucestershire GL50 9RW

Orders: Please visit www.illuminatepublishing.com
or email sales@illuminatepublishing.com

British Library Cataloguing-in-Publication Data

A catalogue record for this book is available from the British Library

ISBN 978-1-911208-88-4

Printed by Barley Print, Cuffley, Herts

07.20

The publisher's policy is to use papers that are natural, renewable and recyclable products made from wood grown in sustainable forests. The logging and manufacturing processes are expected to conform to the environmental regulations of the country of origin.

Every effort has been made to contact copyright holders of material produced in this book. Great care has been taken by the author and publisher to ensure that either formal permission has been granted for the use of copyright material reproduced, or that copyright material has been used under the provision of fair dealing guidelines in the UK – specifically that it has been used sparingly, solely for the purpose of criticism and review, and has been properly acknowledged. If notified, the publisher will be pleased to rectify any errors or omissions at the earliest opportunity.

Editor: Dawn Booth
Design and layout: Kamae Design
Cover design: Nigel Harriss
Cover image: Dinga / Shutterstock

All weblinks are correct at time of going to press.

Answers to the Knowledge Check activities and Check It questions, plus a glossary of key terms, can be found on the Illuminate website at: www.illuminatepublishing.com/AQA_GCSE_Media_RG_Answers.

Contents

Acknowledgements

p1 Dinga / Shutterstock; p5 Bloomicon; p8 Age UK - 'No One Should Have No One'; p11 Monkey Business Images; p12 Doctor Who; p13 (top) Lara Croft GO Launch Trailer / YouTube; p13 (bottom) Kim Kardashian: Hollywood / YouTube; p19 Courtesy of the Advertising Archives; p20 Represent feat. Lady Leshurr / NHS Give Blood; p22 Daily Mirror; p23 doddiss77; p25 Universal Pictures / Learn Online Video; p26 David Tadevosian; p27 (top) Faraways; p27 (bottom) Air Images; p28 (top) Class; p28 (bottom) Khosro; p30 Rabbit Proof Fence; p31 Santipong Srikhamta; p32 Herlanzer; p34 (top) MITstudio; p34 (bottom) Courtesy of Reveal; p35 Courtesy of Reveal; p36 (both) Daily Mirror; p38 Courtesy of the Advertising Archives; p39 (top) I, Daniel Blake; p39 (bottom) Tomb Raider: Underworld; p40 Twin Design / Shutterstock.com; p41 (all) Zoella, Who Run the World?; p42 (top) Atstock Productions; p42 (bottom) REDPIXEL. PL; p43 (top) dennizn / Shutterstock.com; p43 (bottom) Lara Croft GO; p44 NAAN; p45 (top to bottom) IgorGolovniov; Irina Alexandrovna; zffoto; symbiot; lidi Papp; Coffeemill; AlexRoz; Bronwyn Davies; ARTFULLY PHOTOGRAPHER; p46 Narith Thongphasuk; p47 best works; p48 Full Audrey Hepburn Galaxy Commercial / YouTube; p49 Dmitri Ma; p51 Lorenzo Bringheli / Tatler © The Condé Nast Publications Ltd; p55 Fotontwerp; p56 (top) Volodymyr Goinyk; p56 (bottom) View Apart; p57 Pictorial Press Ltd / Alamy Stock Photo; p59 Class; p60 Kathy Hutchins / Shutterstock.com; p61 FULL Audrey Hepburn Galaxy Commercial / YouTube; p62 LStockStudio; p64 FULL Audrey Hepburn Galaxy Commercial / YouTube; p66 Hector / Alamy Stock Photo; p68 Class; p69 wavebreakmedia; p70 Kim Kardashian: Hollywood; p71 (top) Courtesy of Reveal; p71 (bottom) Courtesy of Antique Collecting; p73 (top) Daily Mirror; p73 (bottom) The Times / News Licensing; p74 Zoella, Autumn Haul, Making a Plan & Hair Makeover; p76 (both) Daily Mirror; p79 Trinity Mirror / Mirrorpix / Alamy Stock Photo; p80 cbatson1969; p81 Reproduced with kind permission of D C Thomson Media; p82 FULL Audrey Hepburn Galaxy Commercial / YouTube; p83 OpturaDesign; p84 Lenscap Photography / Shutterstock.com; p85 Isabelle Ohara / Shutterstock.com; p87 Daniel Fung / Shutterstock.com; p88 (top) DisosbeyArt; p88 (bottom) ESB Professional; p90 (top) chrisdorney / Shutterstock. com; p90 (bottom) Benny Marty / Shutterstock.com; p92 Artram; p93 Toria; p95 ImabeBySutipond; p96 (top) I, Daniel Blake; p96 (bottom) Dr Strange; p98 (top) Courtesy BBFC; p98 (bottom) Alexandros Michalidis / Shutterstsock.com; p99 SpeedKingz; p100 (top) eteimaging; p100 (bottom) ra2studio; p102 Tero Vesalainen; p103 Rob Byron; p104 Monkey Business Images; p105 n_defender; p106 One Direction: History; p107 Doctor Who; p108 Class; p110 iko; p112 Humans; p113 Doctor Strange; p114 Courtesy of BARB; p115 Courtesy of BARB; p116 RAJAR; p117 Square Enix; p119 a-image; p121 quinky; p122 Chinnapong; p123 panitanphoto; p124 Steff Hutchinson; p126 Steff Hutchinson; p127 Lenscap / Alamy Stock Photo; p128 Din Mohd Yaman; p130 The Times / News Licensing; p133 (left) Lorenzo Bringheli / Tatler © The Condé Nast Publications Ltd; p133 (right) Courtesy of Reveal; p134 Tatler Media Pack 2018; p137 (all right) NHS Blood and Transplant; p137 (left) Courtesy of The Advertising Archives; p138 (all) FULL Audrey Hepburn Galaxy Commercial / YouTube; p139 (top) Courtesy of The Advertising Archives; p139 (middle) NHS Blood and Transplant; p139 (bottom) FULL Audrey Hepburn Galaxy Commercial / YouTube; p140 Galaxy; p143 (left) Tony Blackburn Radio 1 opening show / YouTube; p143 (Radio 1 logo) Radio1; p143 (right Beats logo) applemusic.tumbl.com / public domain; p143 (right) Nils Jorgensen / REX / Shutterstock; p144 (top) Radio 1; p144 (bottom) applemusic.tumbl.com / public domain; p145 Andrii Kobryn; p147 Sharaf Maksumov; p148 chrisdorney / Shutterstock.com; p149 (left) Arctic Monkeys - I Bet You Look Good on the Dancefloor (Officieal Video) / Domino Recording Co.; p149 (right) One Direction - History (Official Video) / One Direction; p151 (top) © www.ti-mediacontent. com; p151 (bottom) Calvin Harris - Open Wide (Official Video) ft. Big Sean / Calvin Harris; p152 (both) Arctic Monkeys - I Bet You Look Good on the Dancefloor (Official Video) / Domino Recording Co.; p153 (all) One Direction - History (Official Video) / One Direction; p156 (top) Faiz Zaki / Shutterstock.com; p156 (bottom) I, Daniel Blake; p157 Uber Bilder / Alamy Stock Photo; p158 taniavolobueva / Shutterstock.com; p159 (top) I, Daniel Blake; p159 (bottom) I, Daniel Blake; p161 (all) Daily Mirror; p162 (all) The Times / News Licensing; p163 (all) Daily Mirror; p164 (all) The Times / News Licensing; p165 Lenscap Photography / Shutterstock.com; p166 Source: Audit Bureau of Circulations; p167 (top) Daily Mirror; p167 (bottom) The Times / News Licensing; p171 (top) Zoella; p171 (middle) Kim Kardashian: Hollywood; p171 (bottom) Lara Croft GO; p172 Zoella; p173 James Boardman / Alamy Stock Photo; p174 Kim Kardashian: Hollywood; p175 (top) Kim Kardashian: Hollywood; p175 (bottom) oneinchpunch; p177 Lara Croft GO; p179 opturadesign / Alamy Stock Photo; p182 (left) Doctor Who; p182 (right) Class; p184 Doctor Who; p185 Doctor Who; p190 goodluz; p191 Dragon Images; p192 Age UK - 'No One Should Have No One'; p193 Young Dracula; p194 (both) Tomb Raider Movie; p195 Tomb Raider Movie; p197 Ashes to Ashes; p198 Reproduced with kind permission of D C Thomson Media; p199 johavel

A note on QR codes

QR codes are used throughout this book to help you connect quickly and easily to relevant webpages, including videos for some of the Close Study Products (CSPs). The example here will take you to the AQA Media Studies GCSE webpage for subject specific terminology.

You can use QR codes on a tablet or **smartphone**. Depending on your device, you may need a QR code reader app, which you can **download** free from your **app store**. iPhones and iPads with iOS 11 or later can read QR codes directly from the camera without needing an app.

Using either the QR code reader or the camera, point your device at the QR code, so the code is in the centre of the screen. The device should then either take you straight to the webpage in your normal browser or offer you the **URL** and ask you to click OK to take you there.

Introduction

The exam papers – what to expect

Assessment objectives

The assessment objectives for the two exams and the NEA are:

Assessment objectives		Weighting of AOs (%)			Overall weighting
		Paper 1	Paper 2	NEA	
AO1	Demonstrate knowledge and understanding of: • the theoretical framework of media • contexts of media and their influence on media products and processes.	20	10		30
AO2	Analyse media products using the theoretical framework of media, including in relation to their contexts, to make judgements and draw conclusions.	15	25		40
AO3	Create media products for an intended audience, by applying knowledge and understanding of the theoretical framework of media to communicate meaning.			30	30
Overall weighting of components		35	35	30	100

Media One is slightly more weighted towards knowledge and understanding, while Media Two is more weighted towards analysis.

In both exams you will need to show that you are able to:

- Recall the information you have learned during the course.
- Draw together information from the different areas of the course.
- Apply your knowledge and understanding to the questions set, including analysing **media products** you haven't seen before.
- Analyse and compare products to show how they communicate **meanings**.
- Write answers that show your knowledge and understanding of **media issues**.
- Use specialist subject-specific terminology appropriately.

Both papers will ask you to demonstrate and use your knowledge and understanding of the areas of the **theoretical framework, historical, social, cultural** and **political contexts** for the **media**, and to analyse **media products**.

Media One

Media One is divided into two sections:

- Section A covers **Media Language** and **Media Representations**, testing your knowledge and understanding of any two of:
  - **magazines**
  - **advertising** and **marketing**
  - **newspapers**
  - **online, social and participatory media** and **video games**.
- Section B covers **Media Industries** and **Media Audiences**, testing your knowledge and understanding of any two of:
  - **radio**
  - **music video**
  - **newspapers**
  - **online, social and participatory media** and **video games**
  - **film** (industries only).

Some of the questions will be about your CSPs.

You will have an **unseen source** in the paper and some of the questions will be about that product. You are not expected to know about the product already. You will be using the analysis skills from your GCSE Media Studies course to write about the **Media Language** and **Media Representations** in that product. There could be further **unseen sources** elsewhere in the two exam papers.

Tip

The paper will contain at least one **unseen source** – a **media product** that has not been set as a CSP, which can be reproduced in print form within the exam paper.

IMPORTANT NOTE

Updated information on the CSPs is published each year by AQA. It is possible that some CSPs may be removed and replaced, so it is important that you check to make sure you are working on the current CSPs.

There will be some short-answer or multiple-choice questions that are worth 1 or 2 marks. There will also be questions requiring mid-length and longer responses. One question in Media One will have 20 marks available; this is likely to be the final question on the paper. It is an extended response question – your answer should show that you can construct and develop a logical, relevant and sustained argument, and use examples to illustrate what you are saying. The front of the paper will remind you about this, with wording such as:

Question x requires an extended response. You will be assessed on the quality of your written response, including the ability to construct and develop a sustained line of reasoning which is coherent, relevant, substantiated and logically structured.

Media One Section A – Media Language and Media Representations

There will be questions on any two of the following **media forms**, including the relevant CSPs:

- **magazines**
- **advertising** and **marketing**
- **newspapers**
- **online, social and participatory (OSP) media** and **video games.**

An **unseen source** is likely to be used within this section, which could be any **media product** that can be printed, including screenshots from online products or video games. You could be asked a short-answer question about a very specific part of the **media language** or **representation**. You could be asked a longer-answer question asking you to analyse the whole product. You are likely to find both types of question about the **unseen source**.

Knowledge Check 0.1

Short-answer question example:

What is **connoted** by the size and positioning of the woman in this advert for Age UK? [2 marks]

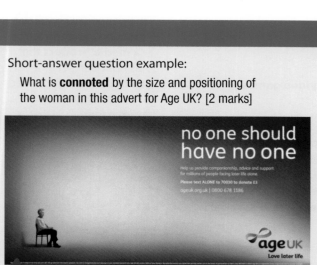

Print advert for Age UK

You may also find print versions of one or more of your CSPs, with related questions. However, questions about the CSPs may not include visual support, so you will need to revise the products themselves to be able to answer them. You will not know which two **media forms** have been chosen for each section of the paper, so ensure you know *all* the CSPs.

Short-answer questions will often test your understanding of terminology, such as the word '**connoted**' in Knowledge Check 0.1. In this example, the **key term** is used within the question, and your answer will show that you understand the terminology. You may also be asked directly what a **key term** means and be expected to provide a definition.

Knowledge Check 0.2

Short-answer question example:

Briefly explain what is meant by the term 'stereotype'. [2 marks]

Longer-answer questions in this section will usually ask you to present an analysis of a product; this could be on an **unseen source** or one of your CSPs. This analysis could focus on a specific aspect such as **narrative** or gender **representation**. It could also be a more open-ended question, giving you the opportunity to choose which elements to discuss. You may have found from your lessons that there can be more than one 'correct' approach and more than one 'correct' answer when you are analysing **media products**.

Knowledge Check 0.3

An analysis question for the Age UK advert on page 8 could be:

Analyse the Age UK advert to show how different elements communicate meaning. [12 marks]

If you had to write a 200-word analysis in response to this, which aspects would you choose to write about?

Media One Section B – Media Audiences and Media Industries

In Section B you will be tested on any two of the following **media forms**, including the relevant CSPs:

- **radio**
- **music video**
- **newspapers**
- **online, social and participatory (OSP) media** and **video games**
- film (Media Industries only).

Again, you will have a mix of short-answer and longer-answer questions. You will be tested on your knowledge of terminology in this section as well as in Section A. Make sure you revise and use the specialist terms in this book – many of them are in **bold** so you can spot them easily.

There is a Subject Specific **Vocabulary** glossary available on the AQA website, at: https://www.aqa.org.uk/resources/media-studies/gcse/media-studies/teach/subject-specific-vocabulary. Or you can use this alternative link to the same page: https://bit.ly/2DHM6Qk.

There is also an online Glossary of key terms on the Illuminate website at: www.illuminatepublishing.com/AQA_GCSE_Media_RG_Answers.

QR code for the AQA Subject Specific Vocabulary glossary

Knowledge Check 0.4

Short-answer question example:

Briefly explain what is meant by **conglomerate** ownership. [2 marks]

In longer-answer questions, you will be assessed on your understanding of the nature of the **media industries** you have studied, and the relationship between **media products**, **producers** and **audiences**. You will need to answer these with reference to your CSPs. Longer-answer questions, especially the 20-mark question, are likely to refer to **contexts of the media**: historical, social, cultural or political. For example, a question could ask about the changing **audience** for **music radio** (**historical context**) with reference to the two **radio** CSPs.

Consider this longer-answer question example, from the first sample AQA Media One paper, where the focus is on **audiences**:

> How are print **newspapers constructed** to address their **target audiences**? In your answer you should refer to the *Daily Mirror*. [9 marks]

Notice that although the question refers in general to 'print **newspapers**', you are also told exactly which CSP to refer to. This means that you are expected to use this one example of a **newspaper** to illustrate points about **newspapers** in general. For example, you could make a general point that **newspapers** use specific styles of **vocabulary** and lengths of sentences to suit the preferences of their **target audiences**, and could then refer to the short and punchy sentences in your CSP edition of the *Daily Mirror*, and how these are suitable for the target demographic of that **newspaper**.

Media Two

Media Two focuses specifically on the in-depth CSPs, although **newspapers** and OSP/**video games** are in-depth CSPs that could *also* feature in Media One. Media Two is divided into two sections:

- Section A will be based on television and will start with a screening from one of your two television CSPs.
- Section B will be based on **newspapers** or **online, social and participatory media** and video games.

Media Two Section A – television

Instead of an **unseen source**, at the start of this paper you will have a screening of an extract from one of your television CSPs, and you could be tested on any area of the theoretical framework in relation to this extract. You will be given two minutes at the start of the exam to read through the questions in Section A, so that you are aware of these before you watch the extract.

You will have studied the full episode in class during the Media Studies course but will only see about three minutes of the episode during the exam. You will see the extract twice, with a five-minute gap between the screenings. During this whole time, you can make notes on what you have seen. Altogether, the screenings and note-taking could take up about 15 minutes of the 90-minute exam. There will be a space in your exam answer book to write your notes. Once the second screening has finished, you can start to answer the questions.

There will be some questions that are about the television programme in general, which might ask you to refer to the other television CSP as well. There will be other questions that ask for direct analysis of the extract you have just seen. You may be making notes during the screenings in order to answer more than one question. The sample AQA Media Two paper has two questions that refer directly to the extract, and two others on the television CSPs.

In the two minutes before the extract is shown, you can use the time to make sure you understand exactly what the questions on the television CSPs are asking, and which one(s) should be answered solely in relation to the extract.

Tip

Use this two-minute period to highlight the **key words** in the questions as this will help you to focus your attention while watching the extract.

This will be made clear in the wording of the question. This could include phrases such as 'how is this demonstrated in the extract?' or 'how is this **constructed** in the extract?', or 'in an analysis of the extract'. Alternatively, the question could ask you to answer with reference to the full named episode(s). Make sure you check this carefully, as you will not be rewarded for any examples drawn from elsewhere if the question relates only to the screened extract. Also use this time to interpret the questions for yourself, putting them into your own words if it makes them clearer for you.

For example, a question on the sample AQA Media Two paper says:

'**Narrative** features grab and hold the **audience**'s attention.' How far does an analysis of the extract of 'Co-Owner of a Lonely Heart' show this to be true? [12 marks]

Let's look at this question in detail.

You can see that you are being asked about the *extract* only, so you know that you shouldn't be referring to details from within the rest of the episode, nor from the other television CSP.

Before you see the extract, you might want to remind yourself what '**narrative** features' means. You will be looking for elements within the extract that move the story forwards. This could include the **representation** and actions of the characters, the way they interact, and the function of them within the storyline (you might see something related to **Propp**'s theories). You could also look at how obvious the main **plotline** is within this segment, any sense of threat or **conflict** to disrupt the **equilibrium**, and the use of **enigma**. Or perhaps you might focus on the use of editing to create clarity or confusion.

The question asks about how these features 'grab and hold the **audience**'s attention', so you are not only going to be discussing the **narrative** features themselves, but you should also write about how the **audience** will respond to each aspect you mention. Will this aspect help the **audience** be sucked into the storyline, and want to watch more, or will it be somehow off-putting? Although you're not referring to details from the rest of the episode, you are expected to know where this extract fits into the **narrative** as a whole, so if it is, for example, the opening **sequence**, you could refer to how it sets the **audience** up for the rest of the episode.

Finally, the question asks how far you think this extract shows the statement to be true. You are being asked for your conclusion, backed up by evidence from the extract. You can agree that in this extract the **narrative** features do grab and hold the **audience**'s attention, or you can disagree and say that they don't. Both answers are acceptable, as long as you give good reasons based on specific details from the extract. Although this is the final part of the question, it does not mean you should answer it only at the end. Instead, the question is inviting you to make judgements *throughout* the answer as you write about each '**narrative** feature'.

After reading through the paragraphs opposite, you should be able to see that your answer could be much longer than you have time and space for – remember, this is an example of a 12-mark question. The AQA sample question paper has allowed about a page and a half for the answer. This is why we are referring to the questions as 'open-ended'. No-one is expected to write about every possible aspect. In your answers, write about what you consider to be the most relevant details in support of the opinion you are putting forward.

Media Two Section B – newspapers *or* online, social and participatory media and video games

In Section B you will answer questions on either **newspapers** or **online, social media and participatory media** and **video games**. Remember that the specific products assessed by this paper are all 'in-depth CSPs' so you could be tested on any area of the theoretical framework, as well as the **contexts**: **historical**, **social**, **cultural** or **political**. Longer-response questions will tell you which CSPs you should refer to.

The final question on the paper will be a **synoptic question**, for which your answer will need to draw together your knowledge and understanding from across the full GCSE Media Studies course. This question will also ask you to refer to at least one of your CSPs.

As with the extended response question in Media One, you will be expected to make judgements and draw conclusions, using relevant examples from your CSPs to support what you are writing.

Consider this example of a longer-answer question from Section B of the first sample AQA Media Two paper:

> 'Gender **representation** in video games is fair and balanced.' How far do you agree with this view? Your answer should refer to Kim Kardashian: Hollywood and Lara Croft GO. [20 marks]

Although the question asks specifically about **representation**, it would be possible to also discuss **audience** and industry to some extent. You might refer to these aspects to explain how and why the different **representations** within the games have been **constructed**. As with the **newspaper** question discussed on page 11, you will use the named CSPs as examples to make more general points about the question – in this case about gender **representation** in video games. You could make a general point about different **character types** being appropriate to different **genres** of games, no matter what gender they are, then refer specifically to the differences between the **representation** of Kim Kardashian in the Hollywood simulation game, and Lara Croft in the GO adventure puzzle game.

Lara Croft GO (top) and Kim Kardashian: Hollywood (bottom)

Question stems

There is a list of command words used in AQA Media Studies GCSE exams, and their meanings, at https://www.aqa.org.uk/resources/media-studies/gcse/media-studies/teach/command-words.

Assessment objectives	Typical question stems	What you are being asked for
AO1 1a Knowledge of the theoretical framework of Media Studies.	Which one of these … Identify … What is … What does this **denote** … What do these **connote** … Briefly explain … Briefly state …	Factual information A definition To recognise what '**denote**' or '**connote**' mean
AO1 1a/1b Knowledge of the theoretical framework of Media Studies. Demonstrate understanding of the theoretical framework of media.	Explain how … Briefly explain … Explain … Why do … How … Explain why …	To apply your knowledge of the relevant aspects of language, **representation**, **audience** and industries to the question.
Plus AO2 1b Make judgements and draw conclusions.	How far is this true … How far do you agree …	As above, plus giving your opinion with evidence and reasoned argument to back it up.
AO1 2a/2b Demonstrate knowledge of contexts of the media and their influence on media products and processes. Demonstrate understanding of contexts of the media and their influence on media products and processes.	Explain how …	To apply your knowledge of the relevant aspects of **social**, **historical**, **cultural** and **political contexts** to the question.
Plus AO2 1b Make judgements and draw conclusions.	To what extent is this true? To what extent …	As above, plus giving your opinion with evidence to back it up.
AO1 1b Demonstrate understanding of the theoretical framework of media. AO1 2b Demonstrate understanding of contexts of the media and their influence on media products and processes. AO2 1b Make judgements and draw conclusions.	How far do you agree …	To apply all your understanding of Media Studies and give your opinion with evidence to back it up.

Assessment objectives	Typical question stems	What you are being asked for
AO2 1a Analyse media products using the theoretical framework of media, including in relation to their contexts.	Analyse … to show … Analyse … How is this done … How are these represented … How … How is … demonstrated?	To carry out an analysis of the **media** product referred to in the question.
Plus AO2 1b Make judgements and draw conclusions.	How far does … show this to be true? How far is this true …	As above, plus giving your opinion with evidence to back it up.

Attaining higher grades

Higher grade marking criteria include:

- Excellent knowledge and understanding of contexts and their influence on **media** products and processes, demonstrated by consistently effective discussion/explanation of [the issue specified in the question].
- Excellent knowledge and understanding of the theoretical framework, demonstrated by consistently effective discussion/explanation of [the issue specified in the question].
- Excellent analysis of the product(s) detailed and critically engages with the nuanced aspects of [the issue specified in the question].
- Consistent appropriate and effective reference to [the issue specified in the question].
- Consistent appropriate and effective focus on the intended **meanings created** by the [e.g. *different elements of* media language].
- Excellent use of the theoretical framework that demonstrates a detailed and accurate understanding of [the theoretical aspect specified in the question].
- Excellent, astute judgements and conclusions that are consistently well supported by relevant examples.
- Consistent appropriate and effective use of the theoretical framework throughout.
- Consistent appropriate and effective use of subject-specific terminology throughout.

In other words, to gain high grades, you need to:

- show excellent knowledge and understanding of **media** studies
- focus on the set question and the **media** products that are asked about
- include your balanced judgements backed up with evidence
- use subject-specific terminology.

There is no reference in the marking criteria to the number of points you need to make in an extended response, or to the overall structure of your answers. The emphasis is on the *quality* of your answer.

1 The theoretical framework and analysis

Introduction to the theoretical framework

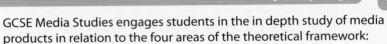

Spec Spotlight

GCSE Media Studies engages students in the in depth study of media products in relation to the four areas of the theoretical framework:

- media language
- media representations
- media industries
- media audiences.

Rapid Recap

You will need to revise all four areas thoroughly. There are chapters in this book on each of the four areas, covering the relevant **key terms** and knowledge for each one.

Media Language (page 21) – the building blocks of any **media** product, such as **camera shots**, **sounds**, colours and **fonts**, and the ways these are used to **create** and **communicate meanings**.

Media Representations (page 58) – how the **media** portray (or *re*-present) events, **issues**, individuals and **social groups**.

Media Industries (page 84) – how **media** products are **financed**, created, marketed, distributed and regulated.

Media Audiences (page 103) – how the media target and address **audiences**, how **audiences** react to the **media** and how some members of the **audience** create or interact with media products.

You have studied each of your Close Study Products (CSPs) in relation to one, two or all four of these areas.

Links

Also see **Media Language** pages 8–45, **Media Representations** pages 46–86, **Media Audiences** pages 87–109 and **Media Industries** pages 110–152 in the student book.

Media form	CSPs for 2019/2020	Language and Representations	Industries and Audiences
Magazines	*Tatler* front cover *Reveal* front cover	✓	
Advertising and marketing	Galaxy TV advert NHS Blood and Transplant online video OMO print advert	✓	
Radio	Radio 1 launch day, Tony Blackburn Julie Adenuga, Beats 1 Radio		✓
Music video	Arctic Monkeys 'I Bet You Look Good on the Dancefloor' One Direction 'History'		✓
Film*	*Doctor Strange* *I, Daniel Blake*		*Industries only
Television	*Doctor Who*, Episode 1 *Class*, Episode 4	✓	✓
Newspapers	For examination in 2019: *Daily Mirror*, Wednesday 15 March 2017 *The Times*, Wednesday 15 March 2017 For examination in 2020: *Daily Mirror*, Wednesday 5 May 2018 *The Times*, Wednesday 5 May 2018	✓	✓
Online, social and participatory media	Zoella Kim Kardashian	✓	✓
Video games	Kim Kardashian: Hollywood Lara Croft GO	✓	✓

The contexts of the media

Spec Spotlight

This specification requires students to closely analyse and compare media products in relation to relevant key social, cultural, historical and political contexts.

Media products should be considered in the light of the contexts in which they are produced and received.

Tip

The exams are assessing your understanding of these four areas, using the CSPs as case studies. In most cases, ideas you have learned in relation to one CSP can also be applied to other CSPs.

For each of your Close Study Products you will have learned about some of these contexts. These are revised in the relevant sections for each CSP:

- **Social contexts**: society's **attitudes** and dominant opinions at the time the product was created. How closely does the product reflect (or **subvert**) the **values**, **attitudes** and expectations of the **audience**, both at the time of **release** and when considered today?
- **Cultural contexts**: these include how a **media** product fits in with other **media** produced at the same time. How closely does the product reflect (or **subvert**) other products and their content? What is the cultural **significance** of a **media** product when viewed by **audiences** and critics?
- **Historical contexts**: what was going on in the world when the product was created? How does the product reflect the time it was produced?
- **Political contexts**: the impact of **government regulation** and influence on the **media**, and the contrasting political perspectives on **media** issues.

Tip

For each **media** form, you have studied two or three CSPs. The contexts are usually different, which gives you a way to start comparing them.

Analysing media products

Knowledge and understanding should be developed through the practical analysis or creation of media products.
- AO2: Analyse media products using the theoretical framework of media, including in relation to their contexts, to make judgements and draw conclusions.

Communication theory

Tip

Forty percent of the marks available for the GCSE overall will be awarded for the quality of your analysis of media products: both **unseen sources** and your CSPs. You need to practise your analysis skills with as wide a variety of products as you can.

Linear models of communication:
- sender
- message
- receiver.

- A **medium** is a channel of communication.
- The **media** are the main channels of communication.

In order for communication to take place there must be:

- a sender: the **media producer**
- a message: the content of the **media product**
- a receiver: the **audience**.

The **media** are the means by which the **producers** get their messages to us; for example, via a **website**, television programme or a **magazine**. Increasingly, however, the **media** are **interactive** so the **audience** can send messages back to the **producers**.

Semiotic analysis

Spec Spotlight

Fundamental principles of semiotic analysis, including connotation and denotation.

Rapid Recap

When carrying out an analysis, you will be using **semiotics**. **Semiotics** is the study of **signs** and their **meanings**.

The **signs** – things you can see and/or hear in a **media product** – are combined together using codes that enable us to understand them.

Each **sign** has a **signifier** – the thing we see or hear – and something **signified** – the meaning of the **sign**.

The **denotation** is the literal meaning of the **sign**. The **sign denotes** what it actually is.

The **connotations** are the potential **meanings** of the **sign** that you have learned through your experience of wider culture. The **sign connotes** some deeper **meanings**.

In this OMO advert from 1955 (one of your CSPs), the **denotation** in the main **image** is of a woman looking over her shoulder while hanging out her washing. The **connotations** are that she is about to talk to the viewer in a friendly way, and that she is very happy with the quality of her wash.

- **Anchorage**: if the intended **meanings** of a **sign** in a **media** product are not clear, they can be **anchored** by the use of further **signs** or codes. This could be by adding a **caption** to an **image**, putting two visual **signs** next to each other, or adding a **voiceover narration** over **moving images**, for example.
- **Icon**: a **sign** that looks or sounds like the thing it refers to. For example, a photograph of a bear is an **icon** of a bear.
- **Symbol**: a **sign** that doesn't look or sound anything like the things it refers to, so we need to have learned its **meaning**. For example, a red rose is a **symbol** of romance.

Link

The chapter on **Media Language** (pages 21–57 of this book) revises these codes in greater detail.

You will need to use your knowledge and understanding of **Media Language** and **Media Representations** to carry out an effective analysis. You may need to relate these to your knowledge of **Media Audiences** and **Media Industries**.

Knowledge Check 1.1

Screenshot from 'Represent featuring Lady Leshurr'.

1   What is **denoted** in this **screenshot** from 'Represent featuring Lady Leshurr'?

2   What is **connoted** by the **background** and the **juxtaposition** of the featured man with the **background**?

3   In this **advertising** CSP, what helps to **anchor** the **meanings** of this **image**?

Tip ✓

To carry out an effective analysis, you need to be able to spot the **signs** and suggest their potential **connotations** for their **target audience**. You may also have to say how the contexts of the **media** have affected these **signs** and their **meanings**.

2 Media Language

Spec Spotlight

Students should have knowledge and understanding of how the media, through their forms, codes and conventions, communicate meanings. Students will be required to demonstrate knowledge and understanding of how media products reflect the social, cultural, historical and political contexts in which they are produced.

The construction of media products

Spec Spotlight

How choice (selection, combination and exclusion) of Media Language elements influences meaning in media products to create narratives, to portray aspects of reality, to construct points of view, and to represent the world in ways that convey messages and values.

Rapid Recap

Media products are **constructed** by **selecting** and combining elements of **Media Language**. Each element – such as a colour, **camera shot** or **sound** – is a **sign** that conveys a **meaning**. When these **media** product elements are combined, the **meanings** become increasingly clear. On their own, each aspect of **Media Language** could have several **meanings** – they could be **polysemic** – but the **meanings** are **anchored** by putting the aspects together.

Link

For more on Media Language see Chapter 1 of the student book.

Tip

The assessment criteria refer to 'appropriate and effective use of subject specific terminology' throughout both the sample exam papers. Key terminology is in bold throughout this book to help you remember and use these terms. Definitions for these **key terms** can be found in the online Glossary at www. illuminatepublishing. com/AQA_GCSE_Media_ RG_Answers.

Knowledge Check 2.1

What have the **newspaper's producers** used to **anchor** the **meanings** of the **headline** and photographs in the **double page spread** from the *Daily Mirror* below?

Identify as many aspects of the **layout** as you can using specialist terms, then look at page 36 of this book to see if you were right.

Advertisement for an internet provider was in this space.

Codes and conventions

Spec Spotlight

The 'rules' of media language: how signs are selected, deselected and assembled to conform to codes and make meanings.
The constructed nature of reality.

- The codes and conventions of media language, how they develop and become established as 'styles' or genres (which are common across different media products) and how they may also vary over time.

Rapid Recap

Codes are systems of communication. For a code to work it needs:

- **Signs**: things we see or hear.
- Rules: the ways in which **signs** can be organised. These become the **conventions** within each **media format**.
- **Shared understanding**: the people sending and receiving the code both need to understand it. For example:

Sign	Rules	Shared understanding
Image of person standing behind a podium on a stage.	Published as the main image on the **front page** of a **newspaper**.	This **image** must be linked to an important news story and is likely to be an influential person (e.g. a politician) making a speech.

The **media** use a range of codes in their products to help the **audience** understand the **meanings**.

Conventions are established ways of combining **Media Language** to create **media** products, such as **newspapers** having a **masthead** across the top of the **front page** and a photograph with each major story, or **websites** having a **navigation bar** or **icon**. **Conventions** make the products easier to understand quickly, as the **audience** quickly learn where to expect them, but these are more likely to be taken for granted than formally stated.

As well as having common **conventions** to allow their **audiences** to understand them more easily, **media** products also need a **unique selling point (USP)** to make them different from other similar products, in order to attract an **audience** to buy, watch, listen, play or read them.

Tip

The **conventions** of each **media format** can change gradually over time. If you are asked to compare two **media** products from different decades, you should be able to discuss these changes.

Knowledge Check 2.2

What are the main **conventions** of a **newspaper front page**?
Check your response by looking at page 36 of this book to see if you are correct.

Varieties of code: Technical codes

Spec Spotlight

Varieties of code:
- Technical.
- Verbal and non-verbal.
- Symbolic.
- Design, layout, typography.

Link

See also 'Technology and media products' on page 54 of this book.

Rapid Recap

Technical codes are the ways in which the available equipment and technology for a given **media form** are used to convey **meanings**. As **media** technology is constantly evolving, so the **technical codes** associated with different **media forms** change and develop. For example, **TV dramas** in the 1960s were made with large, heavy cameras that were difficult to move, so the range of **camera shots** and **camera movements** used in them was more limited than today. Current **TV dramas** often have **hand-held** Steadicam shots and overhead **bird's eye view shots** of outdoor **scenes**, filmed using drones.

Photographic codes 1

Rapid Recap

The following **technical codes** are used within both **still image** and **moving image** photography.

- **Composition**: how the elements in an **image** are arranged within the **frame** – the rectangular border of the photograph or **moving image**.
- **Dominant signifier**: the part of the picture that carries most **meaning**.
- **Foreground**: the part of the **scene** nearest the camera.
- **Background**: the part of the **scene** furthest from the camera.
- **Middle ground**: the part of the **scene** between the **foreground** and **background**.
- **Rule of thirds**: the most important elements are placed a third of the way across or a third of the way up or down the **image**.
- **Headroom**: a small **space** left above the head (or highest part) of a person, so they are not cramped within the **frame**.
- **Leading room**: more **space** is left in front of a moving person than behind them, to give them room to move into.
- **Depth of field**: the amount of the **scene**, from front to back, that appears to be in focus:
  - **Shallow depth of field**: only a small distance from the camera is in focus, the rest of the **image** is blurred.
  - Deep focus: the full distance of the photograph is in focus.
- **Crop**: how an **image** is trimmed at the edges, to lose unwanted parts.

Rule of thirds grid: the important elements of the image should be placed on the lines for aesthetic effect, as shown in the film still below.

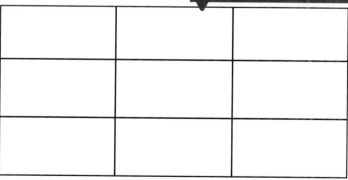

Knowledge Check 2.3

Use as many of the terms on page 25 as you can, to write a description of this **image**.

Tip

You may not have time or space to write about all the codes within an exam analysis. Choose the ones that you think carry the most **meaning**, relevant to the question asked. Explain how and why they create this **meaning**.

Photographic codes 2

Rapid Recap

The following are also **technical codes** associated with photography and **moving image** work.

Shot types

Shot sizes are easiest to think of in terms of portraits of people, but also apply to other subject matter. They describe how large the subject is within the **frame**, or how much of the subject you can see.

- **Extreme close-up (ECU)**: a small part of a face or body. Used to show detail.
- **Big close-up (BCU)**: the main features of the face. Used to show emotion.
- **Close-up (CU)**: head and shoulders. Used to show emotion or intense dialogue.
- **Medium close-up (MCU)**: head to mid-chest. Used to show dialogue.
- **Mid-shot** or **medium shot (MS)**: head to waist or hips. Used for news broadcasters and to show what a character is doing with their arms – giving some sense of action.
- **Long-shot (LS)**: head to feet. Used to show a character moving, or show where they are.
- **Wide angle (WA)** or **extreme long-shot (ELS)**: a wider landscape shot. If people are present, they are not big enough to fill the full height of the **frame**. Used to show a **location**.
- **Camera angles**: used to describe where the camera is placed in relation to the subject.
- **High angle**: the camera is above the subject, looking down. This suggests that the subject is weaker than the viewer or the implied viewer.
- **Eye level**: the camera is level with the most important part of the subject (e.g. a person's face). This suggests equality between the subject and the viewer.
- **Low angle**: the camera is below the subject, looking up. This suggests that the subject is powerful.
- **Canted angle** or **Dutch tilt**: the camera has been rotated slightly sideways, looking diagonally. This can suggest that something is wrong, such as a person being drunk, or can make an **image** seem livelier.

High angle (top) and low angle (bottom) camera shots

Camera lenses

- **Fish-eye lens**: ultra-wide-angle **lens** that can cover 180˚ and curves the view, particularly at the edges. Used to create distorted views, often in **music videos**.
- **Telephoto lens**: magnifies the subject matter, making it appear closer.
- **Wide-angle lens**: as the name suggests, this takes in a **wide angle** of the **scene**, meaning you can squeeze more of the **space** into view. This makes parts of the **scene** seem further away.

Lighting

- **High-key lighting**: the **scene** has even lighting throughout, so everything can be seen. Typically used in **genres** such as rom coms, sit coms and soap operas.
- **Low-key lighting**: the **scene** has pools of light and deep shadows, so some things are hidden. Typically used in **genres** such as horror, adventure and science fiction.
- **Dramatic contrast**: describes a **scene** with **low-key lighting**, where the difference between the shadows and the lit areas is very obvious.

 Tip

In an analysis, as well as using the correct term for a **camera angle** or **shot size**, make sure you say why this particular one has been used. To help you to do this, think about whether a different view of the same **scene** would have been as effective.

Knowledge Check 2.4

Select the relevant terms from those on page 27 to describe this image.

Still image from BBC Three's *Class*: 'Co-Owner of a Lonely Heart', Episode 4.

Moving image codes 1

Rapid Recap

All of the **photographic codes** on the previous three pages also apply within a **moving image** product such as a TV programme, film or online video. However, there are other additional codes within these **media forms**.

More shot descriptions

A reaction shot

- **Establishing shot**: a **wide shot** or **extreme long-shot**, used to establish where an event is happening. Most typically used at the start of a **sequence** of shots.
- **Over-the-shoulder shot**: used mostly in **dialogue sequences**, shot as if from over the shoulder of one character, looking towards another character. The shoulder of the first character may or may not be seen in the shot.
- **Point-of-view (POV)** shot: filmed as if from the **point of view** of one of the characters within the **narrative**.
- **Reaction shot**: showing one character's reaction to something that has happened or has been said. Usually comes straight after a shot of the event or another character speaking.
- **Two-shot**: simply a shot that includes two characters, usually because they are doing something together.

Camera movements

- **Crab**: the whole camera moves on a dolly diagonally to the side, typically to gradually reveal more of the **scene** or to follow an action.
- **Crane shot**: the camera is sited on a crane or drone to allow it to rise or fall.
- **Dolly shot**: the whole camera is moved on wheels, often towards or away from the subject. Used in preference to a **zoom** in TV or film drama, as it looks more natural.
- **Hand-held**: the **camera operator** moves freely with the camera, giving a shaky feel to the **footage**.
- **Pan**: a fixed camera rotated left or right, to sweep across a **scene**.
- **Steadicam** or steady cam: the camera is mounted on a counterweighted device (**hand-held** or strapped to the operator) that stabilises the camera. This allows the **camera operator** to move freely with the camera but gives a smoother final effect than hand-holding it.
- **Tilt**: a fixed camera tilted either up or down, often to emphasise how high or low something is.
- **Tracking shot** or **track**: the whole camera moves on a dolly on tracks or moves as if on tracks. Often used to follow someone or follow an action.
- **Whip pan**: a very quick **pan** across a **scene**, to quickly move attention from one point to another.
- **Zoom**: created with a fixed camera, using the **lens** to make the subject appear to move closer (zoom in) or further away (zoom out). Rarely used in TV or film drama, as it draws attention *to* the use of the camera and *away* from the **narrative**.

Tip

You are studying the following **media forms** that include **moving image**: film, **music video**, television, **advertising** and online **media**. You are *not* expected to specifically study the **media language** used in film or **music video**.

Knowledge Check 2.5

The 19-second **trailer** for *Class*, Episode 4, available on YouTube at https://www.youtube.com/watch?v=KZ944218YPA, has just over 20 shots. Can you describe the first ten, using photographic and **moving image codes**?

QR code for *Class* **trailer** on YouTube.

Shot number	Shot size	Camera angle	Camera movement (if any)	Other shot description (if any)
1				
2				
3				
4				
5				
6				
7				
8				
9				
10				

Moving image codes 2

Editing

Most fictional products are shot using **continuity editing**, which is designed to be invisible. If it is done well, you should not notice it. **Continuity editing** involves creating a **sequence** of shots that conveys a continuous sense of an action or event. **Sound** is an important element in helping the **audience** to believe the **sequence** is real.

Continuity editing must also follow two rules:

- **180˚ rule**: imagine a line drawn across the **set**. The camera must stay on one side of this line. It can only move within a 180˚ arc. This keeps the **background** and the direction of the action the same throughout the **scene**.
- **30˚ rule**: the camera must move *at least* 30˚ between consecutive shots. This avoids having **jump-cuts**. These are edits between consecutive shots taken from the same position or similar positions. The **scene** and the action appear to **jump**.

On the other hand, a **montage** is an edited sequence of shots from different moments in a story. This is often used to compress time.

Some **sequences** have specific names depending on their place within the programme:

- **Title sequence**: includes the **title graphics** announcing the name of the programme and can include other credits.
- **Pre-title sequence**: used in some films and TV programmes to introduce characters or actions before the titles.
- **Cold opening**: usually a **pre-title sequence** that jumps straight into the action, involving the **audience** as soon as possible.
- Cliffhanger: ending **sequence** that leaves the **audience** wanting to know what will happen next.

Edits/transitions

A range of different techniques can be used to change from one shot to the next:

- **Cut** or **straight cut**: an instant change between two shots. The most commonly used edit, which implies that time is continuous.
- **Fade in**: a shot gradually emerges from a blank (usually black) screen. Used at the beginning of a **sequence** or **scene** to show it does not directly continue from the previous **scene**.
- **Fade out**: a shot gradually disappears leaving a blank (usually black) screen. Used at the end of a **sequence** or **scene**.
- **Mix/dissolve**: one shot gradually merges into the next. Can suggest a passage of time, or that two different events are happening at the same time.

Tip

You will have to analyse a specific **sequence** from one of your television CSPs, which will be screened in the Media Two exam. See page 11 for ideas about the best way to make notes during the screenings.

A dissolve transition is used in the film *Rabbit Proof Fence*.

Other editing techniques

- **Cross-cutting**: switching alternately from events in one **location** to another, showing that they are happening at the same time.
- Cutaway: interrupting one shot by switching to a view of something else that is usually related. Can hide something from the **audience**, such as a gory moment of impact or an error.
- **Ellipsis**: the omission of a period of time.
- **Flashback**: showing a previous event, often as if it is a character's memory.
- **Green screen** or chroma key: actors are filmed against a green **background**, which is replaced with other **footage** during editing.
- **Shot-reverse-shot**: standard editing technique for a **dialogue sequence**, typically moving alternately from one **over-the-shoulder shot** to the other.
- **Slow motion**: suggesting that time has slowed down.
- **Time lapse**: suggesting that time is moving quickly.

Actors are filmed against a green screen.

 Knowledge Check 2.6

a. What is the difference between a **sequence** that uses **continuity editing**, and a **montage sequence**?

b. What is the difference between a **title sequence** and a **pre-title sequence**?

c. What is the difference between **cross-cutting** and a cutaway?

d. What is the difference between a **cut** and a **dissolve**?

Audio codes

 Rapid Recap

Sound for moving image

The **sound** in a **moving image** product, such as a television programme, can carry just as much **meaning** as the images, and can help to direct your attention to specific details on screen.

You will need to be able to use the following terms:

- **Soundtrack**: the combined **sounds** of the film, video or television programme.
- **Diegetic sound**: **sound** produced from within the action on the screen, from within the world of the film or programme (this world is the '**diegesis**'). **Diegetic sounds** include:
  - Dialogue: spoken conversation between characters.
  - **Foley sounds**: these recreate the **diegetic sounds** of important actions on the screen but are created by **foley artists** in a studio.
  - **Wild sound/atmos/ambient sound**: the background noise in any **scene**, which can help to suggest the **location**.
- **Non-diegetic sound**: **sound** that would not be heard within the world of the film or programme. **Non-diegetic sounds** include:
  - **Music**: where this is added to create a mood or atmosphere.
  - **Voiceover**: a voice not really present in the **scene**, such as the interior thoughts of a character or an external narrator explaining what is happening.

A **sound editor** or **sound mixer** will add these different layers of **sound** together, **foregrounding** some to make them louder and direct the viewer's attention to whatever is making the **sound**. This can also be called **heightened sound**: when a **diegetic sound** is made unnaturally louder.

A sound mixer at work

Sound for radio and podcasts

Although **radio** and podcasts will use some of the same **sound** sources as **moving image**, there are also some **sounds** specific to these **media forms**:

- **Jingle**: a catchy tune that advertises a **radio** station, **presenter** or product.
- **Music bed**: both **radio** and **advertising** use **music beds** in the background, to evoke an atmosphere or mood; usually instrumental pieces, relatively low in volume, allowing other **sounds** to be clearly heard.
- **Sponsor tags**: short, pre-recorded pieces giving the name of the sponsor.
- **Stab**: a very short ident, only 1 to 3 seconds long, with the name of the station and music or a **slogan**.
- **Station ident**: the name (and often the frequency or **URL**) of the **radio** station, spoken or sung, to let listeners know which station they're tuned in to.

Phone-ins and **interviews** have specific **conventions**, with the **radio presenter** acting as the host, asking the questions and being able to stop a guest in mid-flow to move on to something new.

Voices on **radio** can be differentiated by their accent, **pitch** and **pace** of speaking. All of these help the **audience** to form an idea of the person who is doing the speaking.

Tip

For **radio**, you are studying **audience** and **industries**, *not* **language** and **representations**. However, you might wish to refer briefly to a specific element of a **radio** show to explain how it **targets** the **audience**.

Knowledge Check 2.7

Find the Galaxy 'Audrey Hepburn' television commercial (CSP) online and listen to the **soundtrack**.

What **sounds** are used? Which are **diegetic** and which are **non-diegetic**?
What **meanings** do each of the **sounds** add to the **images**?

Print codes: Design, layout and typography 1

Spec Spotlight

Varieties of code:
- Technical.
- Verbal and non-verbal.
- Symbolic.
- Design, layout, typography.

Rapid Recap

Print design has (at least) three functions: attracting the viewers' eyes to make people want to read; allowing the **audience** to locate the genre or sub-genre of the product and therefore its purpose; and making the content on the page easy to understand. The following **technical codes** are used to do this:

- **Colour palette**: the range of colours available to the designer. Designers usually choose a limited **colour palette** (e.g. only using red, black and grey). Remember: different colours have different **meanings**.

- **Juxtaposition**: ('juxta' = near) placing two **design elements** next to each other so that each influences the other's **meaning**. This could reinforce or contradict the original **meaning** of each element.

- **Layout**: how the different **design elements** are arranged on the page.

- **Superimposition**: ('super' = above or over) laying one element of the design on top of another, so they overlap.

Link

See page 45 of this book for more on the **meaning** of colours.

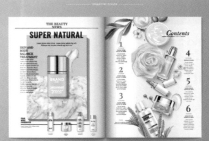

Magazine design for a double page spread: the images on the left page are placed on a **grid**. Those on the right have been tilted to give a more **dynamic** look.

- **White space**: the use of **space** around and between the **design elements**, to allow them to be seen separately. The **space** does not have to be white.

- **Design elements**: can be uniformly placed in a horizontal and vertical **grid** (**formal** and neat) or can be tilted to look more **informal**, **dynamic** and eye-catching.

- **House style**: a common design style to the pages within a **magazine** or **newspaper**, using similar colours, **fonts** and **layouts**.

- **Serif** and **sans serif fonts**: a **serif font**, such as Times New Roman, has a small decorative line or 'foot' (called a serif) added to most letters. A **sans serif font** ('sans' = without), such as Verdana, is much simpler. **Serif fonts** look traditional and authoritative. **Sans serif fonts** look more modern, friendly, **informal** and possibly more youthful.

- **Upper case** and **lower case** letters: **upper case** letters are capitals. A whole word in **upper case** has more impact but is harder to read at a glance. **Lower case** is more friendly.

Knowledge Check 2.8

Write a brief description of this **front cover** of *Reveal* **magazine**, using as many of the terms above as you can.

The front cover of *Reveal* (CSP)

Tip ✔

In the exam you will have to analyse at least one **media** product that you haven't studied as a CSP. Being able to use the correct terminology from this chapter of the revision guide will help you to write accurately about what is **denoted** (shown) – you will also need to suggest the **connotations** (underlying **meanings**) of each element, relevant to the question being asked.

Print codes: Design, layout and typography 2

Varieties of code:
- Technical.
- Verbal and non-verbal.
- Symbolic.
- Design, layout, typography.

Rapid Recap

Let's look at some of the specific elements of **magazines** and **newspapers**.
Some of those used on a **magazine front cover** are:

Cover price

Logo

Main **image** (cut out)

Cover story

Splash head (all caps)

Small **image**

Cover line

Edition/date

Buzzword

Superimposition

Pull quote

Teaser

Plug

Graphic features

Barcode

The elements used on the **front page** and **double page spread** of a **newspaper** include:

- Strapline
- Dateline/edition
- Website
- Price
- Masthead
- Teaser/plug (**ear** advertisement if it is a **commercial** advert)
- Splash
- Photo/**image**
- Incentive
- Cover story/article
- By-line
- Headline (full caps)
- Lead/**lead paragraph** (with **5Ws**)
- Body
- Standfirst
- Small **image** (cut-out **image**)
- Jump/jumpline

- Folio
- Dateline
- Boxed story
- Strapline
- Copy
- Headline
- Columns
- Main **image**
- Standfirst
- Superimposed **image**
- Graphic features
- Caption
- Buzzword
- Panel
- By-line
- Graphic feature
- Lead
- Body
- Pull quote
- Single **column** story

A **magazine** or **newspaper** could also include a **standalone (image)** – an **image** not related to a major story on the same page, or possibly not even related to a major story in the same issue. The photo and its **caption** tell the story.

Both **newspapers** and **magazines** use **section heads** to help readers know where they are in the issue. Each **section** may have several **articles** (or stories). A long **article** may be split down into the main **body copy** and other separate **panels** or boxed copy, such as **fact boxes**.

Newspapers also include:

- **Breaking story**: a story that appears in the news for the first time.
- **Op-ed**: an opinion **column** opposite the editorial page, written by a named columnist.
- **Photo-story**: a **newspaper** story that is more important than it would otherwise be because it is accompanied by an interesting photograph.
- **Running story**: a news story that appears for two or more consecutive days.

Tip

You will almost certainly not have time to write about everything you can see in, or remember about, a **media** product. Always read the question carefully, plan what point(s) you want to make in your answer, and then decide which features of the product best illustrate those points.

Knowledge Check 2.9

Write a paragraph describing the **layout** of any of the **newspaper** and **magazine** products discussed in this chapter, using some of the terms from this and the previous pages. What does each element you write about add to the **meanings** for the **audience**?

Print codes: Design, layout and typography 3

Spec Spotlight

Varieties of code:
- Technical.
- Verbal and non-verbal.
- Symbolic.
- Design, layout, typography.

Rapid Recap

Let's look at some of the specific features of print **marketing** products such as **print adverts** and DVD or **video game** covers.

Subheading
Logo
Graphic feature
White space
Body copy
Slogan

Headline
Main **image**
Pack shot/ product shot

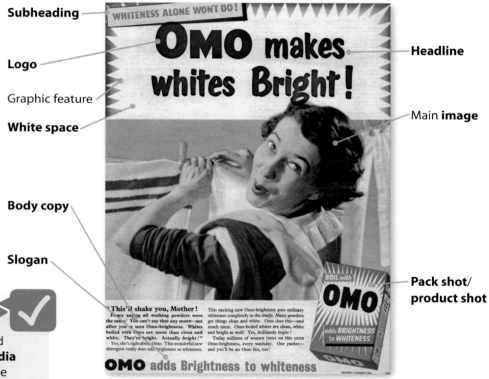

Adverts often follow the acronym **AIDA**:

Attention: make people notice the advert.

Interest: make people want to know about the product or service.

Desire: make people want to have (buy) the product or service.

Action: tell people how to act on the advert to get the product or service.

They use specific **design features** to create each of these stages of their intended impact on the **target audience**.

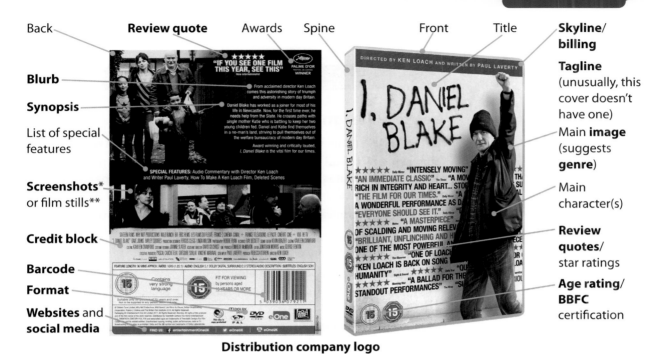

Back	**Review quote**	Awards	Spine	Front	Title	**Skyline/ billing**

Blurb

Synopsis

List of special features

Screenshots* or film stills**

Credit block

Barcode

Format

Websites and **social media**

Tagline (unusually, this cover doesn't have one)

Main **image** (suggests **genre**)

Main character(s)

Review quotes/ star ratings

Age rating/ BBFC certification

Distribution company logo

***Screenshots** are captured from the finished film.

****Film stills** are usually taken by a **stills photographer** on the **set** while the film is in **production**. They can be specially posed to encapsulate a key moment from the film, using the same **mise-en-scène**.

Knowledge Check 2.10

Can you label the different elements of this video game cover?

Electronic media codes 1

Rapid Recap

Website design

Each **website** is made up from a series of individual but linked webpages.

Some of the **technical codes** found in photographs and print products also apply to **websites**, for example the use of limited **colour palettes** and different **font** styles.

The following **technical codes**, however, are specific to **website** design:

- **Blog**: derived from 'weblog', a **website** or page updated regularly, in the form of an online diary or **magazine**.
- **Blog post**: a single update on a **blog**.
- **Comment**: post by a reader below a **blog post**, online news item, **social media** post, etc.
- **Embedded content**: any files that have to be pulled into a **website**, separate from the coding, so includes **images**, video and audio.
- **Homepage**: the opening page of a **website** if you type in just the main **domain name** or **URL** of the site.
- **Landing page**: strictly speaking, this is the first page a visitor to a **website** lands on when they click on a **link** to the site, so it could be the same as a **homepage**. **Landing page** is also used to refer to a **standalone** page that visitors go to when they click on an offer; designed to gather their email address before allowing them to access the offer.
- **Links**: allow the visitor to move from one webpage to another, either in the same site or on a different one.
- **Logo**: a **symbol** used to represent a specific **brand**. May include words but can be purely pictorial or abstract in design.
- **Social media icons**: **logos** for Twitter, Facebook, etc. Used across all **media forms** to indicate their **producers** can be accessed via **social media**.
- **Footer**: the area at the bottom of every page that stays consistent from one page to another. Usually contains extra **links** within the site and contact information.
- **Header**: the area at the top of the page that stays consistent from one page to another. Includes the **logo** and navigation menu.
- **Meme**: a video, **image** or piece of text (usually funny) that is copied and shared by internet **users**.
- **Sidebar**: a column at the side of a webpage, for 'extra' information or navigation.
- **Slider**: a slideshow of **images** that automatically replace each other, usually towards the top of the webpage.
- **Sticky header** or **fixed header**: a **header** that stays at the top of the screen when the user scrolls down.

Tip

The **embedded content** in a webpage is just as important as the **copy**, often more so. Make sure that you are aware of how **embedded content** is used to convey **meanings** in your online CSPs.

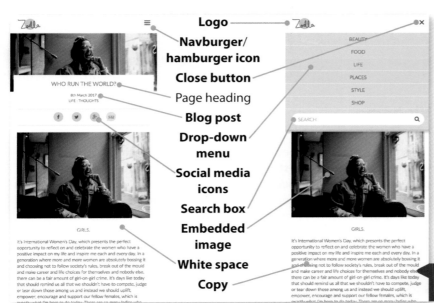

Logo

Navburger/
hamburger icon

Close button

Page heading

Blog post

Drop-down
menu

Social media
icons

Search box

Embedded
image

White space

Copy

Elements of a webpage
viewed on a **mobile device**.

A webpage viewed on a PC.

Knowledge Check 2.11

Look at the two different versions
of the Zoella **webpage**, screen-
grabbed from two different **devices**.
Describe the differences between
them, using **media** terminology.

Electronic media codes 2

Rapid Recap

Vlogging

Vlog is an abbreviation of video **blog**. **Vlogs** are on a specific type of **website**, or section of a **website**. They obviously use the main **technical codes** of **websites**, but the **vlog posts** – the videos created to go on the **vlogs** – use other **technical codes** in addition. These include the general **technical codes** of **moving image** forms (see pages 28–32), but there are also some specific **conventions** less often seen in other **moving image** products:

- **Jump-cuts**: cuts between shots taken from the same or similar angles, showing that some time has been missed. This suggests that the vlogger turned off the camera or edited out some mistakes at this point.

- **On-screen graphics**: drawing, writing and diagrams, often on top of the video **footage**, adding information to it.

- **Outtakes**: errors made during filming, which are revealed to the **audience** often at the end of the 'proper', fully edited version of the video.

- **Rewinds**: running a section of the video again, sometimes after seeing it run backwards at high speed.

- Titles: these are normally more in-your-face and appear more frequently than in other video products.

Video games

Just like **vlog posts**, video games use many of the **technical codes** of **moving image** products. Because they are fully **interactive**, they have some codes of their own:

- **Assets**: the building blocks of a game, including characters, objects, **sound** effects, **music** and **environments**.

- **Avatar:** character within the game that represents a gameplayer.

- **Background**: the visual layer of the game behind the action that brings visual appeal and **meaning** but doesn't affect **gameplay**.

- Character: person or animal (etc.) within the game that can move and affect **gameplay**.

- **Controls**: anything that can be used to make the events in the game happen, including hardware **controls** (keyboard, console controller, etc.) and on-screen **controls**.

- **Cut-scene**: a video showing the next part of the story, created using the game software rather than video software.

- **Gameplay**: the actions that have to be taken by the player, and their effect on the characters or situation.

- **Interactive element**: an **asset** within the game that the player can use or affect.
- **Intro movie**: a short video that sets the start of the game's **narrative** before **gameplay**.
- **Level**: a stage within the game. Players have to complete the challenges within each **level** before moving on to the next **level**.
- **Location/environment**: where the game is set. The **environment** can determine some of the limits to **gameplay**.
- **Objectives**: what the characters or gameplayers are trying to achieve.
- **Obstacles**: problems the characters will encounter that must be overcome.
- **Power-up**: an object that a character can use to increase their skills or capabilities.
- **Prop**: any **asset** that characters can use within the game; can often be collected or altered by the player.
- **Sound**: it is obvious what **sound** is, but video game **sound** includes **alerts** or clues about the gameplay.
- **Sprite**: a small **bitmap graphic**, such as a character or object, that is designed to be used within a larger **scene**.

 Knowledge Check 2.12

Identify as many of the codes above as you can in this screengrab from Lara Croft GO, as well as any relevant codes from **moving image** or photography.

✓ **Tip**

Longer response questions will usually be more open-ended, allowing you to focus on whatever is most relevant. However, they are likely to include 'prompts' that direct you towards certain aspects that you must include in your answer. Shorter response questions – for 1 or 2 marks – might focus on very specific aspects of **Media Language**, for example asking about the **denotation** or **connotations** of one element of a product.

Varieties of code: Symbolic codes

Spec Spotlight

Varieties of code:
- Technical.
- Verbal and non-verbal.
- Symbolic.
- Design, layout, typography.

Rapid Recap

As mentioned at the start of this chapter, many of the **Media Language** elements are **symbols** that convey **meaning**. **Symbols** are **signs** that have **meanings** because of a **shared understanding** of our culture, such as the full moon **signifying** a scary mood in a horror movie. In this context, the **image** of a full moon is a **symbol** because it doesn't physically look like the **meaning** ('scary') that we attach to it.

These **signs** and **symbols** can be put together within the **mise-en-scène**, a French term meaning 'put in the **scene**'. All the elements you can see should have been included deliberately to communicate specific **meanings**.

Mise-en-scène includes the following features (CLAMPS):

- **C**ostume
- **L**ighting, **location**
- **A**ctors and actions
- **M**ake-up and hair
- **P**rops
- **S**et and set dressing.

Each one of these elements can suggest something about the characters, their situation and their lifestyle.

Colours can be used symbolically, although the **meanings** are not always the same for each colour. The precise **meanings** will be **anchored** by other codes within the **media** product.

A full moon can signify a scary mood.

Knowledge Check 2.13

As objects, people and animals can be **symbols** in our shared **media** culture, fill in the blank column in the table opposite, to show what potential **meanings** could be conveyed in a **media** product by the main content of each photograph.

Image	Colour	Potential meaning of colour	Potential meaning of content
	Black and white	Timeless, classic, old-fashioned, historical	
	Sepia	Old, memories, nostalgia	
	White	Innocent, child-like, ghostly	
	Black	Scary, death, evil	
	Red	Danger, lust, blood, romance	
	Green	Natural, healthy, environmentally friendly	
	Blue	Cool, calm, logical, scientific	
	Gold	Classic, royal, luxury	
	Rainbow	Childhood, happiness, gay pride, diversity	

Sound can also be used symbolically. Horror films use the following **sounds** to **connote** a sense of imminent threat: creaking floorboards, owl hooting or thunder, for example.

Symbolic codes are usually dependent on the **audience**'s **shared understanding** of them because they have seen or heard them before. Without this **shared understanding** the **symbols** fail to convey a **meaning**.

Tip

Symbolic codes can be interpreted by **audiences** in different ways. This is often because **audiences** have different cultural experiences. In an exam response, you should be able to analyse the **symbolic codes** in a **media** product in terms of the *range* of potential **meanings**.

Varieties of code: Verbal and non-verbal codes

Spec Spotlight

Varieties of code:
- Technical.
- Verbal and non-verbal.
- Symbolic.
- Design, layout, typography.

Rapid Recap

Verbal codes are about words – verbal means 'of language'.

Characters in films and TV programmes use specific **vocabulary** (words) and **syntax** (ways of putting words together) to indicate something about their personality, situation or background.

Newspapers and **magazines** make specific word choices to **position** the **audience** in relation to an issue, event or person.

Non-verbal codes are about the way people dress, move and act, and about the way they say things:

- The way people dress includes their clothing, hairstyle, body adornment and accessories.

- The way people move and act includes the way they walk, run or dance, their facial expressions, head movements and gestures, and how close they get to other people.

- The way people say things – their **paralanguage** – includes their tone of voice, their pitch, volume and **pace** of speaking (or shouting).

The **audience** understand these codes because of their experience from being with a variety of people, and because of their previous experiences with **media** products and wider culture.

Shot sizes and **camera angles** often emphasise specific **non-verbal codes** to ensure the **audience** notices them.

Tip

When carrying out an analysis, look for the combinations of different codes that help to **anchor** the **meanings** of each one. Explain how they work together within the **contexts** of the **media** product to reinforce each other.

Knowledge Check 2.14

What do the **non-verbal codes** in this **image** convey to the **audience** about the people and the situation?

Genre

Spec Spotlight

The codes and conventions of media language, how they develop and become established as 'styles' or genres (which are common across different media products) and how they may also vary over time.

Theoretical perspectives on genre:

- principles of repetition and variation
- the dynamic nature of genre
- hybridity
- intertextuality.

Rapid Recap

Genre = category or type.

In the **media**, each product within a **genre** will share codes and **conventions** with other products in the same **genre**.

For example, the leading **film genres** in terms of ticket sales are: adventure, action, drama, comedy, thriller/suspense and horror.

Genres can be related to:

- Content: films and TV programmes are grouped by content, as in the **film genres** above.

- Function: **social media** sites are grouped by how people use them, such as video sharing, photo sharing, instant messaging or chat-based, and blogging **platforms**.

- **Audience**: **newspapers** are grouped by their readership, although they are referred to by labels such as tabloid/red top/popular or black top/mid-market or broadsheet/quality.

Spec Spotlight

The evolution and development of genres (including hybrid genres) in different media forms.

Rapid Recap

Hybrid genre: combining **conventions** of two or more **genres** to create a new category. For example, One Direction's *History* **music video** combines the **genres** of performance and **narrative**.

Subgenre: a specialist area within a **genre**. For example, Radio 1 is a music **radio** station, but is also mainly a contemporary pop music station.

Each **genre** has its own set of shared codes and **conventions** by which the **genre** can be recognised. Each new product also brings new elements to refresh the **genre**. The introduction of these elements over time allows the **genre** to develop and change.

A **hybrid genre** can emerge that is successful enough to be copied over and over again, and become a new **genre** in its own right.

Spec Spotlight

Intertextuality, including how inter-relationships between different media products can influence meaning.

Rapid Recap

Intertextuality: when one **media** product refers to or borrows from another **media** product or another **genre** that the **audience** are likely to be familiar with.

The Galaxy 'Audrey Hepburn' TV advert (left) shows **intertextuality** by using the style of Audrey Hepburn's films. This gave a sense of glamour to the product because of the association with the Hollywood star.

Knowledge Check 2.15

1   List as many **genres** of **magazines** as you can think of.

Tip ✓

There may be 1 mark or 2 mark questions asking you to define terms such as '**hybrid genre**' or '**intertextuality**'. Don't spend very long on these questions. Sometimes, though, these questions lead on to the next question, setting you up to understand a point that is important in the next task.

2   *Tatler* is a fashion and lifestyle magazine. What are the codes and **conventions** of this **genre**?

Appeal of genres

Spec Spotlight

Factors influencing the creation of genre products:
- financial
- cultural
- audience demand.

Rapid Recap

Media products within recognisable **genres** appeal to **audiences** because:

- they know what to expect
- they find it easy to select products similar to ones they have already enjoyed
- they build up a knowledge and understanding of the **genre**, which helps them to enjoy it even more.

Media products within recognisable **genres** appeal to **media producers** because:

- such products are cheaper to produce because everyone involved already knows what to do
- they are easier to market
- there is an existing **audience**
- there is a lower risk of financial failure.

As long as **audiences** appear to be enjoying and engaging with a **genre**, **media producers** will continue to make products within that **genre**. Using **word-of-mouth**, including sharing on **social media**, **audiences** can increase or decrease the popularity of a **genre** among themselves.

For a **genre product** to be *successful*, it needs to use the accepted **conventions** of the **genre** so that **audiences** get what they expect. It also needs to add something new and unusual, so that **audiences** are surprised and pleased.

Media producers can break – or **subvert** – the **conventions** of a **genre** to create something that looks like it will be familiar, but will then have some very different and unexpected elements.

Presenter hosting a phone-in.

Knowledge Check 2.16

Match the **genre** to the **media form**:

Media form	Genre
Magazines	Horror
Newspapers	Performance
Films	Tabloid
Music videos	Phone-in
Social media	Crime drama
Video games	Lifestyle
Television programmes	Instant messaging
Radio programmes	Role-playing

Tip

If you are comparing two products from different time periods but the same **genre**, such as *Doctor Who*'s first ever episode and *Class*, consider how the codes and **conventions** of the **genre** have changed over time.

Narrative theory

Spec Spotlight

Theories of narrative, including those derived from Propp (character types).

Narrative structure

Spec Spotlight

Narrative development:
- exposition
- disruption
- complication
- climax
- resolution.

Rapid Recap

The **narrative structure** is the way that a story is put together. The story could be factual or fictional. A **narrative** deals with:

- **Causality**: why things happen – in other words, what *causes* each action or event.
- Time: when things happen and in what order.
- **Space**: where things happen.

Most stories can be broken down into the following **narrative** stages:

- **Equilibrium**: the ordinary world of the story, as it exists from day to day.
- **Disruption**: an event or problem that changes the ordinary existence.
- Recognition of **disruption**: the main characters noticing the problem.
- Attempts to restore **equilibrium**: the main actions of the story, as the **protagonist** tries to overcome the problem and put things right.
- New **equilibrium**: the new day-to-day existence after the problem has been resolved.
- The **resolution** is therefore the solving of the problem that disrupted the **narrative**.

Exposition is the filling in of background story details. In TV and film this is often done by having one character discussing events with another character. It could also be done by **flashbacks**, memories or **symbolic codes**. All of these provide clues within the story. This information will be important to understanding the overall **narrative**.

A **complication** is an obstacle in the way of the **protagonist(s)**, the main character(s) at the centre of the story, achieving the **resolution** of the overall problem.

The climax of a **narrative** is the highest point of tension or action, close to the end, when the problem is resolved or the **resolution** is narrowly missed.

There is a specific structure to hard news items in **newspapers**. The opening paragraph usually contains the **5Ws** – Who? What? When? Where? Why? This gives the **audience** the key information about the story.

The next part of the **article** is about 'How?' and fills in further details, potentially including quotes from experts or witnesses. Longer articles end with a pointer towards the future, saying what people expect to happen next. This structure allows an **article** to be **subbed upwards** – cut in length by a **sub-editor**, starting at the bottom of the **article** and deleting sentences until the required length is achieved.

Even a photo or individual print product can contain a **narrative**:

- This may be about time – what has happened, what will happen next?
- It may be about **causality** – why did something happen? Which person or thing did it happen to?
- It may be about a **quest**, such as your own **quest** for happiness, which can be fulfilled by buying a specific product.

Even a print product can contain a **narrative**.

(Image courtesy Lorenzo Bringheli / Tatler © The Condé Nast Publications Ltd)

Knowledge Check 2.17

Consider the three **advertising** and **marketing** CSPs as **narratives**.
Fill in the following table:

	OMO *Woman's Own* advert	Galaxy 'Audrey Hepburn' TV advert	NHS Blood and Transplant online advert
What is the main **disruption** or problem that needs to be overcome?			
Who is the **hero**, or who are the **heroes**, who can overcome the **disruption**?			
Who is the **dispatcher** who sends the **hero(es)** on their way?			
What is the prize/**princess** to be gained by overcoming the **disruption**?			
How does the product or service being advertised fit into this **narrative**?			

Tip

You could be asked to analyse or explain a **narrative** in any type of **media** product.

Vladimir Propp and narrative

Theories of narrative, including those derived from Propp (character types).

Rapid Recap

Vladimir **Propp**'s theory is about the **character types** found in most **narratives**. Many **narratives** can be seen as a **quest**, with a **hero** setting out to conquer a problem in order to win a prize, such as the hand of the **princess** in marriage:

Link

For more on Propp see pages 30–31 of the student book.

- The **hero**: the **protagonist**, the character at the centre of the story.
- The **villain**: the **antagonist** or opponent to the **hero**, who places **obstacles** in the path of the **hero**.
- The **donor**: gives the **hero** a gift to help them on their **quest**.
- The **helper**: the **hero**'s trusted sidekick.
- The **dispatcher**: sends the **hero** off on their quest.
- The **princess**: the reward for a successful end to the **quest**; this could be a person, an object or a desired state such as 'peace'.
- The **princess's father**: the protector of the prize, who can hand it over to the **hero**.
- The **false hero**: mistaken by others as being the **hero**, so makes the **hero**'s **quest** more difficult.

In each case, the term shouldn't be taken too literally – for example, the **princess's father** could be any character, including the **princess** him-/herself, if the **princess** is a person.

Audience appeal of narrative

Spec Spotlight

Audience appeal of narrative:
- enigma
- closure.

Rapid Recap

Narratives appeal to **audiences** because:

- The **audience** can become actively engaged and guess ahead as there is mystery about what will happen – an **enigma**. This gives rise to questions that keep the **audience** thinking about what is going to happen, and makes them want to find out more.

- The best **narratives** misdirect the **audience** to guess wrongly, with the use of clues and **action codes** – **signs** or clues – that suggest what is going to happen.
- There is **conflict** – confrontation. The **conflict** is often between **binary opposites**, such as good v evil, rich v poor. This gives rise to the **complications** for the **hero**. The **audience** enjoys seeing the **hero** succeed.
- There is a sense of closure – the **narrative**'s ending answers all the questions that the **audience** was asking throughout. **Conflicts** are resolved.

Instead of having closure, an individual episode of a **serial** may end with a **cliffhanger**, setting up an **enigma** to be solved in the next episode.

Knowledge Check 2.18

Doctor Who: 'An Unearthly Child', true or false?

	True	False
1 The Doctor is the **hero**.	☐	☐
2 Susan is the **villain**.	☐	☐
3 The teachers are the **false heroes**.	☐	☐
4 Susan's name is an **enigma** at the start of the episode.	☐	☐
5 There is a **conflict** between Susan's knowledge of Science and History, and her knowledge of everyday life.	☐	☐
6 Coal Hill School is part of the **equilibrium** in the **narrative**.	☐	☐
7 The **disruption** to the **equilibrium** is the moment when Susan leaves the school.	☐	☐
8 The discussion between Susan and the teachers about the TARDIS is an example of **exposition**.	☐	☐
9 The **action codes** in the final **scene** suggest a threat to the people in the TARDIS.	☐	☐
10 The episode ends with a sense of closure.	☐	☐

Tip

As **Propp**'s original theory was written in Russian, there are different translations of the labels for the **character types**. Don't worry if you have been taught different words for the same roles. Use the ones you have been taught.

Technology and media products

Spec Spotlight

The relationship between technology and media products.

Rapid Recap

Convergence has two meanings in Media Studies:

- **Media industries converge** – or join together – through **takeovers** and **mergers**.
- **Media forms** merge together as a consequence of **digital technology**.

The prime example of the latter is the **smartphone**, as it allows **users** to play **video games**, access the internet, watch TV, listen to the **radio**, access **social media** and make phone calls.

Link

For more about technological convergence and media language see pages 45–47 of the student book.

Spec Spotlight

How developments in technology impact on content:
- forces that drive technological change
- the impact of new technology on the form, content and meaning of media products:
  - image manipulation
  - high definition
  - user-generated content.
  - computer-generated imagery (CGI)
  - mobile communication technology

Rapid Recap

Technology is constantly being updated by technology companies in order to encourage consumers to buy new goods and services, and to keep ahead of rival manufacturers. **Audiences** also demand technological change, as they notice the problems with existing products.

High definition (HD) video has a higher resolution than standard definition video. This means it has more lines of pixels, which gives a sharper picture. Standard definition has 480 vertical lines in the USA and 576 vertical lines in Europe. Full HD, also known as 1,080p, has 1,080 vertical lines. **Ultra-high definition** video has over 1,500 vertical lines, with the highest resolution currently having 4,320 lines.

Computer-generated imagery (CGI) refers to the use of **graphics software** to generate still or **moving images**. **CGI** is often associated with **animation** and **special effects** in **blockbuster** films but is increasingly being used to enhance conventionally shot **sequences** in **advertising** and television.

The technology affects what is possible and what becomes typical. **Images** are **manipulated** – altered – using software such as Adobe Photoshop®, which can change the **meanings** and/or **representations**.

People no longer expect photographs to always show the truth.

Drones are used for filming overhead shots.

As technology changes, it has an impact on **Media Language**, bringing in new codes and **conventions**. Examples include:

- **Websites** now include **comment** sections at the bottom of many pages.
- Pop-up adverts on the internet increasingly address **users** by name.
- Drones are used, even in low-**budget** TV programmes and films, to create complex overhead **establishing shots** or **action shots**.

User-generated content (UGC) refers to content **uploaded** to the internet by the **audience**, usually videos and **images**. The increase of **UGC** online means both that we are more used to seeing poor quality video and not minding about that quality, and at the same time that we are increasingly the creators of good quality **media products** ourselves.

Much of this content can be created on a **smartphone** or other **mobile device** such as a **tablet**, and uploaded directly from that device, using mobile communication technology.

Knowledge Check 2.19

Convergence question:

Are there any **media forms** that can't be accessed via a **smartphone**?

Tip

You could be examined on four **contexts** for the **media**: **historical**, **social**, **cultural** and **political**. Part of the **historical context** of a **media product** could be the technology that was available at the time it was made, and how this affected the product.

Check It

1 Define the term 'establishing shot'.
2 What does 'polysemic sign' mean, and how can such a sign be anchored?
3 In Media Studies, what does USP stand for?
4 What is the logo banner across the top of a newspaper front page called?
5 What is shallow depth of field?
6 In which genre(s) would low-key lighting most likely be used?
7 What is a two-shot?
8 Name three camera movements.
9 What is the purpose of continuity editing?
10 What is the most commonly used edit?
11 What is a cutaway?
12 Is a voiceover part of diegetic or non-diegetic sound?
13 Is this sentence written in a serif font or a sans serif font?
14 What does 'house style' refer to?
15 What is a pull quote?
16 Where would you find a standfirst?
17 Name three things you would expect to find on the back cover of a DVD.
18 What does mise-en-scène mean, and what does it include?
19 What could embedded content on a website include?
20 What is a vlog?
21 List three assets of a typical video game.
22 What is paralanguage?
23 If someone winks, is this a verbal or a non-verbal code?
24 List as many TV genres as you can.
25 What is a hybrid genre? Give an example.
26 Define the term 'intertextuality'.
27 Why do genre products appeal to audiences?
28 What is exposition in a TV programme?
29 Give two terms for the main character in a TV drama.
30 What is CGI?

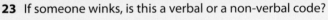

3 Media Representations

Spec Spotlight

- Students should have knowledge of how the media portray events, issues, individuals and social groups.

Re-presenting the world: Truthfulness and realism

Mediation

Spec Spotlight

The ways in which the media re-present (rather than simply present) the world, and construct versions of reality.

Theoretical perspectives on representation, including processes of selection, construction and mediation.

Rapid Recap

Remember that the **media** are channels of communication. They carry the communications of **media producers** to **media audiences**. The **media** re-present the world to the **audience**. As with anyone conveying a **narrative**, it is impossible to convey the *whole* truth of any event or issue, so this is **mediated** – put into words, **sounds** and **images** that give one view of the event or issue. **Mediation** involves both **selecting** and omitting specific information.

Mediation is therefore the process by which a **media** product **represents** an idea, issue, event or group of people to the **audience,** by the use of selection and omission.

Media representations are **constructed** by **media producers**, by choosing and combining **media language** to convey specific **meanings**.

Link

For more on mediation see page 49 of the student book.

Example 1: in a domestic interior in a **TV drama**, the choice of specific elements of **mise-en-scène** can convey information about the personality and lifestyle of the relevant character. In the **image** on the right, the **mise-en-scène** could be characterised as sophisticated but arty and quirky, suggesting that April MacLean has these aspects to her character.

Example 2: in a **newspaper article** about an event, both the choice of facts to include about that event, and the choice of **vocabulary** used to write about those facts, convey a specific view of what took place.

The term 'mediation' also suggests that this process of selection and omission affects the **audience**'s **perception** of whatever is represented by the **media**.

The **mise-en-scène** of this interior from *Class* tells us about the character of April MacLean.

Knowledge Check 3.1

Complete the following table, showing how different **media production roles** are involved in the **mediation** of events, ideas, groups and **issues**.

Media format	Role(s) involved in the mediation process	Choices made by this role
Newspapers	**Editor**	Which stories to include and omit in the **newspaper**.
Newspapers		Which facts to include in a story.
TV documentary	**Camera operator**	
TV historical drama	Set designer	
Radio music programme		Which songs to play.
Video game	Background artist	
Print advert		How the product being advertised appears to the **audience**.
Music video	Director	
Magazines		How much **space** (and therefore importance) to give to each **article**.
Websites	Copy-writer	

Tip

You may be asked either how something has been **mediated**, or how it has been **represented**. In both cases, you should write about the choices that have been made in **constructing** the specific **representation** and the **meanings** that these convey.

Realism

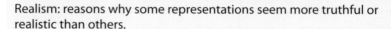

Spec Spotlight

Realism: reasons why some representations seem more truthful or realistic than others.

Rapid Recap

Realism in the **media** doesn't refer to whether something seems like the existing real world, but instead is about whether it is believable as a world in its own right. So a science fiction film or an **animation** about a sponge under the sea can still have a sense of **realism**.

There are four aspects to **realism**:

- **Surface realism**: getting the details right, e.g. not allowing characters on *Game of Thrones* to use a mobile phone.

- **Inner or emotional realism**: characters having an appropriate response, for their given personality, to what is going on around them, e.g. a shy character looks anxious when asked to make a speech.

- **Narrative realism** (plausibility): each action shown or decision taken makes sense within the story that is unfolding, e.g. a scared character runs away from a shocking incident.

- **Technical codes/symbolic realism**: the normal codes of the **media form** expected by the **audience** are being used, e.g. in a science fiction film, a battle in space involves expected **sounds** of lasers and explosions although lasers are silent and **sound** does not carry through the vacuum of space.

If a product does not have all four aspects of **realism**, it seems less 'realistic' or truthful. By **constructing** products that have all four aspects, **media producers** persuade the **audience** to believe their messages.

Knowledge Check 3.2

Watch the Galaxy 'Audrey Hepburn' TV advert online (https://www. youtube.com/watch?v=Z6HKWuZPrdU) and explain how each of the four aspects of **realism** has been used to **construct** the version of reality in this **media** product.

QR code for the Galaxy 'Audrey Hepburn' advert

Still image from the Galaxy TV advert, showing full **mise-en-scène**.

Tip

Always remember that **representations** have been **constructed**, and that each aspect you see or hear is the result of someone's decision-making. You could use words such as 'decision', 'construction' or 'selection' to show that you have understood this.

A window on the world

Rapid Recap

It could be argued that the **media** provide a '**window on the world**' because they bring to the audience **images**, **sounds** and information from places and events around the globe. We could not experience most of these without the **media**. In the **media**-dominated 21st century, it is likely that the majority of our information is gained from the mass **media** rather than from direct first-hand experience.

An argument against this is that, due to the process of **mediation**, we are not simply looking through a window at reality, instead we are seeing a **mediated reality**. The particular viewpoint we are seeing has been **constructed** using selection and omission of information.

Marshall McLuhan coined the phrase 'the **medium is the message**' in 1958. This has been interpreted in two ways:

- Firstly, that (**media**) technologies themselves have an influence on the way we understand and react to their **meanings**. For example, we might read something more quickly and regard it as less important if we read it online than if we read the same information in a printed **newspaper**.

- Secondly, that each new **media form** has an impact on the way we live our lives.

   For the message of any medium or technology is the change of scale or pace or pattern that it introduces into human affairs. (Marshall McLuhan, *Understanding Media: The Extensions of Man,* 1994, Chapter 1)

For example, the introduction of **newspapers** united whole nations, allowing the literate population to know about the same events and people, regardless of their **location**. It could now be argued that the internet, in particular the **smartphone**, has allowed us to live physically more separated from each other, while being more connected intellectually and emotionally.

Knowledge Check 3.3

In the two **newspaper** CSPs, look at the two related stories (i.e. the Muirfield story in the 2019 CSPs or the local elections stories in the 2020 CSPs), and note how each has been **mediated** by the **newspapers'** **production** teams – consider the decisions made by the **journalists** who wrote the stories, the **editors** who decided how prominent the stories should be, the **photographers** and the **layout** designers.

Use this information to argue both for and against the statement that **newspapers** provide a '**window on the world**'.

Tip

Phrases such as '**window on the world**' and 'the **medium is the message**' could be used in extended response questions, where you would be asked to say how far you believed these phrases to be true with reference to specific **media forms** or products. You could approach these questions, as in Knowledge Check 3.3, using evidence from the relevant **media** products to back up your judgements.

Choices within representation

Spec Spotlight

The choices media producers make about how to represent particular events, social groups and ideas.
Audience positioning.
Selective representation, biased and prejudicial representation.

Rapid Recap

- **Audience positioning**: the use of specific **media language** to encourage the **audience** to respond to a **media** product in a particular way. Think of this as nudging the **audience** to take up a particular **position** in an argument about the subject matter – for example, to believe that one character is more innocent than another in a **TV drama**, or to feel angry about a specific issue in the news.

- **Selective representation**: the **media** may only show a limited view of an event, issue or social group, missing out other potential ideas or viewpoints of the same subject matter, e.g. a **newspaper** that supports the government of the day might only include **negative representations** of the leader of the opposition party.

- **Prejudice**: comes from the word 'pre-judge', and refers to the way people make instant decisions about social groups or **issues** before they find out all the information. **Prejudice** can be based on learned ideas, such as those from the **media** or from family and friends.

- **Bias**: a **prejudice** for or against a particular argument, group or individual. News reporting is said to be **biased** if it clearly points to one side of an argument. This can be a **bias** towards a political viewpoint, a social group or just a point of view – for example, if a **local** news report about a festival in a town park only mentions the mess left behind and not the enjoyment gained by, or the money raised for, the **local** community.

All these **media** effects are created by the selection of specific **images**, **sounds**, facts and **vocabulary**.

Tip

When discussing how a specific **bias** or **audience position** has been **constructed**, you could consider both what has been included, and what else could have been included but hasn't.

Knowledge Check 3.4

How does the Galaxy 'Audrey Hepburn' TV advert **position** the **audience** to consider Galaxy to be a glamorous product or to associate Galaxy with a glamorous lifestyle?

Which aspects of **media language** are used to **construct** this specific **representation**?

Representation of reality

The ways aspects of reality may be represented differently depending on the purposes of the producers.

Techniques of persuasive communication.

Advertising, marketing, political bias, propaganda.

Rapid Recap

As the **media** are channels of communication, all **media** products convey a message. Different products have different purposes for their message, including persuading the **audience** about something. Such persuasive purposes include:

- **Advertising**: the use of specially designed **media** products (adverts) to tell the **audience** about specific products and services.

- **Marketing**: the wider promotion of products and services, including the use of **advertising** but also the use of branding, event and **word-of-mouth**. This includes, for example, **interviews** with actors on chat shows, DVD and video game covers, and **music videos**.
- **Political bias**: siding with one political viewpoint.
- **Propaganda**: using the **media** to promote a **biased** viewpoint, usually for political purposes.

In these cases, the **media producers** may **construct** a specific view of contemporary life, in order to persuade the **audience** to act in a specific way – for example, to buy a product, vote for a candidate or take part in a campaign. The **producers** create a **representation** of reality that suits their purposes.

Advertisers often use the acronym **AIDA** to help them **construct** their **media products**:

Attention: the advert needs to attract the attention of the **target audience**.

Interest: the advert must make the **audience** want to know more.

Desire: the advert should make the **audience** want to have the product or service.

Action: the advert should tell the **audience** how to get the product or service.

Tip ✓

Different **audiences** respond differently to **media products**, depending on their previous experiences and knowledge. When writing about a **media producer**'s intended **representations**, remember that not everyone will have understood the messages in the same way, or been persuaded by them.

Knowledge Check 3.5

Identify the persuasive features in this advert.

Advert for Cadbury's chocolate biscuits, from the early 1950s.

Representing people

Some of the choices made to represent people include:

- appearance: age, **ethnicity**, clothes, body type
- voice: accent, volume, **pitch**, choice of words
- behaviour: body language, interactions with others, speed and style of movement
- visual effects: **camera shots**, editing, lighting.

Each of these choices can help to portray a **representation** of an individual personality, or can mark that person as part of a wider **social group**. This could rely on the way the **social group** and their characteristics are **stereotyped** by the **media**.

Stereotypes

Spec Spotlight

The different functions and uses of stereotypes:
- How stereotypes become established.
- How stereotypes may vary over time.
- Positive and negative stereotypes.
- How stereotypes enable audiences to interpret media quickly.

A range of different stereotypes should be discussed and exemplified in order that students understand the problems with and usefulness of stereotypes.

Link

For more on stereotypes see pages 58–60 of the student book.

Rapid Recap

Stereotyping is the reduction of a social group to a limited set of characteristics or preconceived ideas.

A **stereotype** is a **representation** of a **social group** using these limited characteristics.

Stereotypes are usually based on reality to some extent, but with some features of the group ignored and others exaggerated.

People are more likely to **stereotype** groups they don't often come into contact with, and who they perceive to have less power than them. Such **stereotypes** tend to be **negative representations** to some extent. The **media** tend to use the **stereotypes** created by the more powerful groups in society – e.g. politicians, business owners, **media producers** – and tend to use **stereotypes** to portray minority or less powerful groups – e.g. teenagers, minority ethnic groups, old people.

As society changes, and as **social groups** change and become both more or less prominent, their **stereotype** changes. The **representations** linked to these **stereotypes** therefore also change over time. **Stereotypes** are often adjusted as a consequence of campaigns and protests over **negative stereotypes**.

The **media** use **stereotypes** to convey ideas about people (whether individuals or groups) quickly, particularly in 'compact' **media** products such as adverts where there is limited time and **space** to establish a character. The **audience**'s understanding of the **stereotype** enables them to more easily receive the **message** of the advert.

Advertisers will use **positive stereotypes** to encourage the **audience** to buy products in order to be like the people represented.

When new characters are introduced into longer **TV dramas**, they are often **stereotyped** at first, so the **audience** can quickly understand their role in the **narrative**. They then become **individuated**, and less stereotypical, as their character is seen reacting to more situations.

Tip ✓

If you think a character in a **media** product you are analysing has been **stereotyped**, consider why the **media producers** are using this simplified form. What are they trying to convey quickly to the **audience**?

Knowledge Check 3.6

Some viewers have complained that the TV series *Class* used **stereotypes** to create its main characters. Which **social groups** are being **stereotyped** by each of the characters? How have they been **individuated**?

Some of the characters from the BBC Three series *Class*

Tanya:

April:

Matteusz:

Charlie:

Ram:

Corakinus:

Miss Quill:

Tanya:

Social groups

Everyone belongs to different **social groups**, including their family and their friends. Other social groups include clubs, classes, special interest groups and work-mates.

Much larger social groups could be defined by **ethnicity**, religion, **age**, gender, **sexuality** or **social class**. **Subcultural groups** – identifiable groups *within* larger cultures – are defined by shared choices such as manner of dress, musical taste or type of activities. They may label themselves as a group, or be labelled by outsiders. These **subcultures** could include groups such as goths, rock music fans or rugby players.

Social class can be defined by income, groups of occupations or by lifestyle.

The simplest descriptions of **social class** in the UK are working class, middle class and upper class, with lower-middle class and upper-middle class between these three.

The **representation** of each of these groups varies according to the **media producer** and the intended **target audience**.

Social class can be represented by:

- **location**
- clothing
- belongings
- accent and **vocabulary**
- employment
- leisure activities
- interactions with others.

Ethnic groups can be **stereotyped** in different ways, with non-white groups more likely to be represented **negatively** than white groups in societies where power and influence are concentrated in the hands of predominantly white elites. In each country, the immigrant groups to that country are more likely to be **negatively** represented.

Overt racism in the UK **mainstream media** is rare, but minority **ethnic** groups are **under-represented** in most **media forms**. However, it is also the case that some **media** products have challenged **ethnic and racial stereotypes** and made a positive contribution towards undermining wider social **prejudices**.

People with a **sexuality** other than **heterosexual** (members of the LGBT+ [lesbian, gay, bisexual, transgender plus] community) are also **under-represented** in the **media**, although there are notable exceptions to this. Soap operas and youth TV have paved the way for other **media forms**, largely because they want to attract a wide **target audience**, but also because a diversity of characters allows them to develop more interesting **plotlines**.

The **media** will often represent different **age** groups as separate social groups, such as 'teens', 'the elderly', 'baby boomers' (born between 1946 and 1964) and 'millennials' (born between 1980 and 1994, so having their formative years at the turn of the millennium). **Media producers** tend to be aged between about 25 and 55, and **advertisers** prefer to **target** that age group because they are **stereotypically** earning and spending the most. This partly explains why this group is represented the most in the **media**.

Knowledge Check 3.7

In this screengrab from Kim Kardashian: Hollywood, what **signifiers** have been used to represent an upper-class lifestyle?

Tip

The assessment criteria award marks for what you have done well, rather than deducting marks for what you have not done well. Even if you're not entirely sure of an answer, make sure you write a response to every question.

Gender

Spec Spotlight

Theoretical perspectives on gender and representation and feminist approaches.

An exploration of the distinction between essentialist views (that males and females are different categories with essential features, behaviours and attributes that define them) and social constructionalist views that the same features, behaviours and attributes are constructed by society (including the media) and not by nature.

Rapid Recap

- **Essentialism**: the belief that men and women are fundamentally different in terms of their skills, preferences and behaviours.
- **Social constructionism**: the belief that masculine and feminine behaviours are **constructed** by society and not by nature.
- **Feminist theory**: the belief that women and men should be given equal rights, but that society is currently structured so that women are not equal to men.

The **targeting** of some **mainstream media** products and the **representations** of gender within such **media** products rely on more **essentialist** ideas, assuming men and women to have specific roles and attributes. For example:

Male	Female
Stronger	Weaker
Protector	Nurturer
Logical	Emotional
Single-minded	Multi-tasking
Leader	Supporter
Active	Passive

These ideas lead to **stereotypical representations**. For example:

- Men are often represented as having positions of power.
- Women are often shown in skimpy clothing, suggesting sexual availability.

Niche products (aimed at small but loyal **audiences**) can often largely avoid such ideas, as they may not be relevant to their **audiences**.

Feminist theory suggests that the **media** are mostly controlled by powerful men, so report the concerns and views of men more than those of women.

A **feminist analysis** of **media** products also explores how men and women have been represented as having different attributes to each other. It also examines the potential impact these **representations** could have on the **audience** and on their views of men and women.

Front covers of mainstream product *Reveal* magazine and niche product *Antique Collecting* magazine.

There is a gradual tendency in the **media** to move away from more **stereotypical representations**, as society also moves to more acceptance of **social constructionist** ideas and of diversity.

Knowledge Check 3.8

Do you think the following products represent views that tend more to **essentialism** or **social constructionism**? What evidence can you find in the product that suggests this?

- The OMO advert from *Woman's Own*, 1955.
- The Galaxy 'Audrey Hepburn' TV advert.
- The NHS Blood and Transplant online advert.

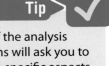

Tip

Some of the analysis questions will ask you to focus on specific aspects of **representation**, such as gender. A good approach would be to include both an explanation of the **meanings** conveyed about that aspect, and an explanation of how **media language** has been used to **construct** those **meanings**.

Viewpoints, values and beliefs, and the significance of representations

Spec Spotlight

How representations (including self-representations) convey particular viewpoints, messages, values and beliefs, which may be reinforced across a wide range of media products.

Role of individuals as producers (as well as consumers) of media messages in which the self is represented.

Contrast between dominant representations and contested representations of, for example, groups, issues and places.

Rapid Recap

The **ideology** of a **social group** is their shared set of beliefs and **values** – ideas about what is right and wrong. In each society there is a **dominant ideology** – the set of ideas and beliefs that is accepted by most people within that society.

Each **media** product also communicates an **ideology**, as it conveys ideas about what is right and wrong, and what is considered important. This means that each product either reinforces or challenges the **dominant ideology** in a society.

Cultural hegemony is the notion that the powerful groups in society have power over the culture of that society, and persuade other **social groups** to perceive their point of view, their interests and their **values** as being natural and common sense. The **media** play a role in this process, by representing the views and cultural interests of the powerful groups as being 'normal'.

Dominant representations: media **representations** of individuals, **social groups** or **issues** that reflect the **dominant ideas**, **values** or **ideology** of a society. **Dominant representations** are built-up through repetition over time until they appear self-evident – the same ideas are conveyed by different **media** products, reaffirming a view seen elsewhere by the **audience**.

For example, both of these **newspapers** (CSPs for examination in 2020) used photographs of Theresa May that reflected the **dominant representation** of her in the **media** during the period of Brexit negotiations – that she was trying hard but was socially awkward.

Representing the self: with the increase in **user generated content (UGC)** people are involved in creating **representations** of themselves, for example within their **social media** profiles and posts. People often use these **representations** to either reinforce or deliberately

> Double page spreads from the *Daily Mirror* and *The Times*, 5 May 2018 (CSPs for examination in 2020).

Tip ✓

When you analyse a section of one of your TV CSPs for the Media Two exam, you will be shown a clip that is approximately three minutes long. This is a good length to work with, from any video, as practice for this part of the exam.

challenge the **dominant ideologies** of their society. For example, beauty vloggers such as Zoella reinforce the notion that looking attractive is important, and that this relies on the use of commercial products.

Contested representations: **media representations** that are *not* accepted by all sectors of the **audience**. These are often based on **dominant representations**, but in such cases the **audience** *notice* that there is a **biased** view, which they react against. Hollywood depictions of countries and people beyond the Americas often prove controversial with non-Americans, such as the depiction of the previously Tibetan character, The Ancient One, in the film *Doctor Strange* (played in the film by white female actor, Tilda Swinton).

Knowledge Check 3.9

Watch a three-minute excerpt from Zoella's **vlog** dated 13 September 2018, called 'Autumn Haul, Making a Plan & Hair Makeover', at https://www.youtube.com/watch?v=aXssvyOtozo.

To what extent is Zoella **reinforcing dominant representations** of women in this **vlog**? What evidence can you use to illustrate your response? How could a vlogger challenge these **dominant representations**?

QR code for Zoella's 13 September 2018 **vlog**.

The significance of representations

The social, cultural and political significance of particular representations in terms of the themes or issues that they address.
Agenda setting.
News values.

Rapid Recap

Agenda setting

Print **newspapers** still seem to lead the main political and social conversations in the **media**, 'setting the agenda' for what the other media products will be discussing. This then leads to conversations about the same topics in political and business circles and in society at large.

Because **newspapers** still set the agenda, their **representations** of a person or issue matter. The selections made and the **biases** these selections have created help to set the way a subject is discussed – including what is considered to be important about the issue.

Moral panic

Moral panic can be seen as an over-reaction by society, fuelled by the **media**, to specific **negative representations** in the **media**. A group or issue is **represented** as a threat to the accepted norms, **values** and interests of society – it is seen as a **folk devil** that has been **demonised** by the **media**. This creates public concern, which is fed by more coverage in the **media**, creating more concern. Often the authorities (e.g. the government or the police) are forced to act, which further reinforces the negative view of the original issue.

Link

For more on moral panic see page 83 of the student book.

News values

News values are used by news **production** companies to decide on the importance of each news story. Each news broadcaster, news site or **newspaper** will have its own set of **news values**, depending on their overall **ideology**. There are some general **news values** that all providers agree on:

- **Bad news**: is more **newsworthy** than good news. In other words, it is more likely to be included.
- Timing: recent stories are more important than older stories:
  - **running stories**: updates on stories that the **audience** are already familiar with
  - **diary events**: calendared events that **news providers** and the **audience** know about beforehand, such as royal visits, sports matches or protest marches.

Tip ✓

For each **newspaper** CSP, you are told to study the **front page** and the selected story (within the context of the relevant page) in relation to **Media Language** and **Media Representations**. In each year's **newspaper** CSPs, the selected story is the same across both the *Daily Mirror* and *The Times*, to help you to make comparisons between the two **newspapers**.

News **article** from the *Daily Mirror* **front page**, 15 March 2017 (top) and 5 May 2018 (bottom).

- **Important people**: celebrities, politicians and royalty are more likely to be covered in a story than other people. Big businesses and the government are also more likely to be covered than smaller organisations.

- Surprise and **significance**: an event that is out of the ordinary will be more likely to be reported on – the larger the impact of the event, the more important it will be. This can include the number of people involved at the time, the severity of the problem or the number of people it could affect in the future.

- **Bias** to home: in a national **news service**, events in that country are considered more important than events elsewhere in the world. Next-in-line are countries with cultural links to the home country or that have international impact, e.g. in UK news, countries such as America, Australia, New Zealand, China and India would be considered important.

- **Human interest**: stories with emotional impact because of the drama affecting real people at the heart of the story. **News providers** also add **human interest** by showing how a major story affects an individual or a small group. For example, after a major earthquake, part of a **news feature** may focus on one child survivor, and detail what happened to them and their family.

The more of these **news values** a story contains, the more likely it is to be covered.

Knowledge Check 3.10 ⚙

Consider each of these news **articles** from the **newspapers** CSPs for examination in 2019 and 2020 respectively. In each case, identify which **news values** are contained within the story.

BY JACK BLANCHARD and NICK SOMMERLAD

FRAUD COPS GRILL TORY MP

Six-hour interview after Daily Mirror probe into alleged election overspending

A TORY MP was questioned by police for six hours over possible election fraud.

Craig Mackinlay, left, was "put through the mill" over his party's alleged failure to declare thousands of pounds of spending in the 2015 general election.

It follows a Mirror probe on 24 Tory MPs and election expenses.

FULL STORY: PAGE 2

SHOWBIZ EXCLUSIVE

CORRIE KEV'S HELD BY COPS OVER BUST-UP

Star, 53, spends night in cells after row but police 'will take no further action'

EXCLUSIVE
BY STEPHEN WHITE

MICHAEL Le Vell has been arrested on suspicion of assault.

The star, 53 – Kevin Webster in Corrie – was treated in hospital after officers were called to his home.

He then spent the night at a Manchester police station, but the force says it will "take no further action".

FULL STORY: PAGE 7

SOAP ACTOR Michael Le Vell

Misrepresentation

Spec Spotlight

How and why particular social groups may be under represented or misrepresented.

Bias and partiality in representation.

Relationship between media representations and the dominant value system of society.

Links

For more on misrepresentation see pages 60 and 80–84 of the student book.

Rapid Recap

- **Under-representation**: the proportion of **media** coverage for a specific group is lower than it should be, given the proportion of that group in the overall population. For example, the vast majority of the main characters throughout the many series of *Doctor Who* have been white, so black and minority **ethnic** (BAME) communities have been **under-represented**, especially those from Asian backgrounds, although more recent series of *Doctor Who* have gone some way towards a more equal **representation**.

- **Misrepresentation**: an individual or group is **represented** in a way that is misleading. It may be based on a very selective group of **signifiers** that tell a limited version of the story. For example, teenagers are usually only mentioned in **newspapers** if they are involved in crime or have done something exceptionally heroic or exceptionally good (for example, achieved highly in national exams). Neither the **negative** nor the **positive representations** suggested are an accurate **representation** of teenagers as a whole **social group**.

- **Fake news**: a deliberate **misrepresentation** of an issue or person, whether this be by emphasising a particular set of facts to give a **biased representation** or by including information that is not true.

There is a tendency in all **media** products for the creators to put people like themselves at the centre of the product – and the majority of **media producers** have traditionally been white middle-class males.

- **Bias:** a **prejudice** for or against a particular argument, group or individual. **Misrepresentation or under-representation** of a **social group** can betray the **bias** of the **media producer** and could potentially lead to further **biased** thinking on the part of the **audience**.

- **Partiality**: **bias** in favour of an individual, **social group**, argument, etc.; could be seen as favouritism. A TV chat show, for example, could show a **partiality** for inviting young, attractive celebrities as guests. Similarly, a **newspaper** may give prominent and favourable coverage to television programmes screened by a company that shares the same owner as the **newspaper**.

Tip

For any question that asks you to analyse a **media** product, a good approach would be to focus on how **meanings** have been **constructed** in line with the concepts introduced in this chapter.

- **Dominant value systems**: sets of ideas, attitudes and beliefs that are shared by most people within a given society. They also determine what is most valued by those people (e.g. honesty, family, security, finance or power).

- **Mainstream media representations**: tend to match the **dominant value systems** in a given place at a given time, but can also help to shape them, as the **media** form part of the shared culture of that society. **Misrepresentations** in the **media** can therefore feed into and shape the **value systems** of a society.

Link

See also **moral panic** on page 75 of this book.

Knowledge Check 3.11

Match the term to its definition.

Term	Definition
Ideology	Dominance over a society's culture by the powerful members of that society.
Dominant value system	A set of unwritten rules to decide what is most important in the news.
Cultural hegemony	The mediation of a **social group** or an issue in a misleading way.
Bias	Set of beliefs and values, including a sense of what is right and wrong.
Partiality	**Bias** in favour of an individual, **social group** or argument.
Misrepresentation	The potential impact on society of representing a **social group** or an issue as a threat to the accepted norms and values of that society.
Under-representation	Set of ideas, attitudes and beliefs shared by most people within a given society.
News values	**Prejudice** for or against a particular argument, group or individual.
Moral panic	Emotional impact due to the **representation** of a news story by concentrating on real, individual people.
Human interest	Shown as being lower in quantity than is actually the case.

Social, historical, political and cultural contexts

Spec Spotlight

Students will be required to demonstrate knowledge and understanding of how media products reflect the social, cultural, historical and political contexts in which they are produced. Not every question in every exam series will require the analysis of the four contexts but students will need to be familiar with all of them in relation to a range of media products.

How representations reflect the social, historical and cultural contexts in which they were produced.

Relationship between representation and changing values and beliefs and culture specific values and beliefs.

Rapid Recap

Each of the CSPs need to be studied in relation to the **contexts** in which it was produced. The **representations** within the **media** products reflect these **contexts**. As the values and beliefs of a society change, so do the **media representations** shared within that society. This is partly because the **media** *reflect* what society believes and partly because the **media** *influence* what society believes.

As well as these variations over time, there are also differences in the values, beliefs and **representations** of different societies and within the same society. For example, an American television drama may express values that are broadly acceptable to a US **audience** but which are offensive to viewers in another society with different **cultural values**.

Social contexts

Social contexts are the way people interact with each other and the influence this has. This includes the way they use the **media** as part of this interaction – such as their use of **social media**, how popular TV programmes become the subject of conversation, or how the **media** fit into people's daily and family lives. It also includes the way the **media** reflect the society of the time. To discover the **social context** ask:

- Who created the product?
- Who were the **audience**?
- How and where did they watch/listen to/read the product and why?

Historical contexts

How political and social events of previous years, and the technologies and **media** channels available at the time, influenced **media** products made then, and the **audience**'s understanding of them. This includes the impact on the form of the product (e.g. television in the early 1960s being filmed and broadcast in black and white) and on the content of the product – the **issues** and **social groups** covered and the **representations** conveyed. To discover the **historical context** ask:

- When was the product made?
- What else was happening at the time?
- How has **media** technology developed since the product was made?

Political contexts

Politics is about power and, specifically, about which group holds the power to govern a particular country or area. The **political context** is therefore about who holds power at the time a **media** product is made and **released**, and the relationship between the **media producer** and those in power, as well as the political views represented in the **media** product itself. To discover the **political context** ask:

- Who made the product?
- What was their relationship to those in power (e.g. big business or the government)?
- Why was the product made?
- What ideas does it promote?

The Cybermen in a 1967 episode of *Doctor Who*, filmed in black and white.

The UK political spectrum

Source: cbatson1969 in TES (2018)
https://www.tes.com/teaching-resource/political-spectrum-diagram-11025057#.

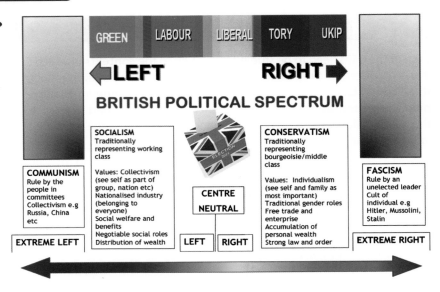

Cultural context

Cultural contexts include the wider culture experienced by the **producers** and **audience** at the time the **media** product was **released**, including arts and entertainment, education, and a society's shared customs, beliefs and attitudes. These cultural experiences influence the way **meanings** are encoded, and the audience's understanding of and reaction to the media product. As the **media** are part of our culture, the **cultural context** also includes how people perceived the **media** form at the time, with television often being seen as 'low brow' (popular but not intellectual or prestigious) culture, and film often seen as slightly more 'highbrow' (prestigious) for example. To discover the **cultural context** ask:

- Where and when was the product made?
- What is/was daily life like for the **audience**?
- Which other **media** products have influenced this product?

Links

See the sections on each CSP in Chapter 7 of this book.

Tip ✓

Sample question:

> To what extent have **social** and **cultural contexts** influenced the **representation** of teenagers in television drama? Answer with reference to the first episode of *Doctor Who*: 'An Unearthly Child' (1963) and *Class*: 'Co-Owner of a Lonely Heart' (CSPs). [20 marks]

You could be asked to show how far any of your CSPs have been influenced by the relevant **contexts** for that product. Make sure you understand the difference between each of the **contexts**, and that you know which **contexts** are relevant to which CSPs.

Knowledge Check 3.12

Look carefully at this **front cover** for clues to its **social** and **cultural context**. Use the questions above about these two **contexts** to help you, as well as:

- What **issues** does *Shout* **magazine** prefer to deal with?
- What are the values and beliefs implied by the choice and the **presentation** of contents illustrated on this **front cover**?

Audience interpretation

Spec Spotlight

The factors affecting audience interpretations of representations including their own experiences and beliefs.
Audience positioning.
Decoding – is the influence of social variables such as age, class, gender, ethnicity on the interpretation of media representations.

Rapid Recap

- All **media** products convey **meanings** to an **audience**.
- **Media producers** encode their **meanings**, using **Media Language**.
- **Audiences** decode the **meanings** when they engage with the **media** product.

Each person who watches, listens to or reads a **media** product has a separate set of existing experiences and beliefs that they bring to that product. These will influence how the person understands and responds to the product. They will use their personal experiences to help them in their decoding. People with different backgrounds and different tastes or political beliefs will respond differently.

Link

See more on audience interpretation in Chapter 5 pages 106–107 of this book.

Audience positioning

Media producers try to control the reactions (or **position**) of the **audience** as much as possible, so that the **audience** understand the **meanings** that were originally encoded. The **media** product will use a specific mode of address – for example, a news report uses an authoritative mode of address and **positions** the **audience** as being willing to learn. A soap opera **positions** the **audience** as being members of the community, who care about other people within the community.

Knowledge Check 3.13

The Galaxy TV advert uses CGI to recreate the Hollywood star Audrey Hepburn as the central character. How would the decodings of the advert be different for:

- older **audiences** who remember Audrey Hepburn's films?
- younger **audiences** who have come to know her films and are fans?
- younger **audiences** who don't recognise her?

Screenshot from Galaxy 'Audrey Hepburn' TV advert.

Tip

If you are asked about **audience response** to a **media** product, consider the make-up of that **audience** and how *they* would respond, rather than assuming *you* are the **audience**. Remember also that there are always various possible ways of decoding a **media** product. All **media** products have a degree of **ambiguity** because the **media language** is **polysemic**.

Check It

1 Define the term 'mediation'.

2 What are the four aspects of realism?

3 What does AIDA stand for?

4 How is a newspaper editor involved in the mediation of the news?

5 What is a stereotype?

6 Why do the media use stereotypes?

7 List three different major social groups.

8 List three aspects that might be used to represent a character's social class.

9 What is 'essentialism' in relation to gender?

10 Define the term 'ideology'.

11 In Media Studies, what does UGC stand for?

12 What is a dominant representation?

13 Is a moral panic a reaction to a negative or a positive representation of an issue?

14 What does the term 'news values' mean?

15 List at least three commonly used news values.

16 How are teenagers misrepresented in the news?

17 Does partiality mean bias *for* or *against* an issue or group?

18 What does the 'historical context' of a media product refer to?

19 Who decodes the meanings in a media product?

20 What does 'audience positioning' refer to?

How do light entertainment shows position their audience?

4 Media Industries

Spec Spotlight

Students should have knowledge and understanding of how the media industries' processes of production, distribution and circulation affect media forms and platforms.

Ownership and Media Industries 1

Spec Spotlight

The nature of media production, including by large organisations, who own the products they produce, and by individuals and groups. Patterns of ownership:

- mergers
- demergers
- takeovers
- concentration.

Rapid Recap

Media industries create **media** products.

Although there are many small-scale **media** companies, specialising in narrow areas of **production**, the **media** are dominated by large, powerful, non-specialist companies. These have been created through:

- **Mergers**: two or more companies joining together to create larger companies. For example, Carlton and Granada TV merged in 2004 to form ITV plc.

The ITV studios in London

- **Takeovers**: when a large company buys up a smaller (usually rival) company or buys enough of its shares to control the smaller company. For example, Square Enix **acquired** Eidos Interactive in a **takeover** deal in 2009, acquiring the Tomb Raider **brand** in the process.

These processes lead to:

- **Concentration of ownership**: when one company or a small number of companies control an increasing share of the market. For example, the different regions of the UK formerly had different companies providing their ITV service. Now all the regions are served by the same company, ITV plc.

- This is also a relatively small-scale example of a monopoly – when one company controls all of a specific area, in this case the 'area' is the ITV channel (Channel 3).

- In the **media industry** as a whole, there are several examples of **oligopoly** – where a market is dominated by a small number of powerful companies. In this situation, the companies tend to cooperate with each other to keep prices high.

- **Demergers**: large companies are broken down into smaller parts, usually because governments restrict the areas of operation of large companies, to prevent too much **concentration of ownership** and to encourage competition.

The headquarters of News Corporation in New York

 Knowledge Check 4.1

Match the term to the **media industry** event.

Term	Media industry event
Merger	Apple launched Beats 1 Radio in 2015 following its **acquisition** of Dr Dre's Beats Music and Beats Electronic.
Takeover	News Corp split off from the major **conglomerate** News Corporation in 2013. The remainder of News Corporation was renamed 21st Century Fox.
Demerger	In April 2018, three pairs of major media industries were looking to combine together: AT&T and Time Warner; Disney and Fox; Viacom and CBS.

 Tip

You are studying **Media Industries** in relation to the following **media forms**: **radio; music video; film; television; newspapers; online, social and participatory media** and **video games**. You need to understand how **media** products in each of these forms are **financed**, created, marketed, distributed and regulated.

Ownership and Media Industries 2

 Spec Spotlight

The effect of ownership and control of media organisations:
- conglomerate ownership
- diversification
- vertical integration
- horizontal integration.

- **Conglomerate**: a group of companies drawn together under single ownership through **mergers** and **takeovers**. A **conglomerate** will have a **parent company** and **subsidiary** companies (or **subsidiaries**).
- **Diversification**: companies often **acquire** other companies or widen their own output in order to **diversify**; that is, to offer a wider range of products and services. For example, Disney bought up Marvel Entertainment in 2009. Traditional Disney films **target** a female **audience** and children. Marvel films **target** a more male **audience** and teenagers. By buying Marvel, Disney also **acquired** its **intellectual property** (the ideas used within their products, such as storylines and characters), so were able to use a wider range of characters and **brands** in their leisure parks, in their video games and on their TV channels.

Vertical and horizontal integration in the Disney conglomerate

Leisure parks and resorts

Film merchandise

ABC Television group, inc. ESPN Inc.
Exhibition: cinema, broadcast and streaming

Distribution and marketing

Walt Disney Animation Studios
Pixar Animation Studios
Marvel Studios   Lucasfilm
Film production

Vertical integration

Horizontal integration

- **Vertical integration**: the **merger** or **takeover** of companies working in different stages of an industry (different parts of the **supply chain**), such as Disney's **acquisition** of the ABC Television group in 1995. This allowed the film-making company to link with American broadcast television, giving it a new outlet for its products.
- **Horizontal integration**: the **acquisition** of companies that are within the same stage of an industry (the same level of the **supply chain**), such as Disney's **takeover** of Pixar Animation or Marvel Studios.

The potential advantages of **conglomeration** for the companies involved include:

- More efficiency, as everything can be done within one overall organisation.
- Lower running costs due to shared resources.
- More **diversification** of products and target **audiences**.
- Higher profits, as there are fewer companies taking a share of the final income.
- Greater **market share** because there are fewer rivals.
- Greater control of the relevant market.

The potential disadvantages of the resulting **concentration of ownership** include:

- Competition is destroyed.
- Too much power is held by too few large companies and individuals.
- There is less diversity of opinion voiced in the **media**.
- The **media** view is distorted to **represent** the interests of the large companies and their wealthy owners.

Disney is the overall owner of the Marvel **brand**.

 Knowledge Check 4.2

Explain the difference between **horizontal** and **vertical integration**.

 Tip

Media One Section B assesses your knowledge and understanding of **Media Industries** and **Media Audiences**. This will include at least one short-answer question, such as asking you to define one of the **key terms** listed in the Specification Spotlights in this chapter. You may also be asked to define terms listed in the glossary of **key terms** (Subject Specific Vocabulary) on the exam board website.

Convergence

 **Spec Spotlight**

The impact of the increasingly convergent nature of media industries across different platforms and different national settings.
Cross media ownership.
Convergence of content providers, network providers and platform providers.

 Rapid Recap

Convergence refers to:

- The ways in which **media industries converge** because of **mergers** and **takeovers.**
- The ways in which **media forms** merge together because of **digital technology**.

For example, Bauer Media owns the **multimedia brand** Kerrang!, which includes the original **magazine** of that name as well as the **radio** station and TV channel. Through **digital convergence**, these platforms can share some of the same content.

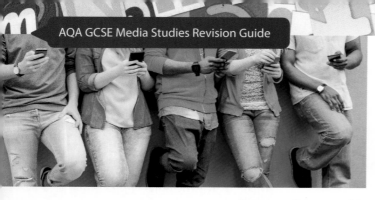

Due to the possibilities of **digital convergence**, and the threat from rival providers online, many **media** providers now offer an online experience related to their offline content. For example, the **national** daily **newspapers** all have online **news services**, and the terrestrial free-to-view TV channels all offer online catch-up or on-demand **streaming services**.

- Cross-media ownership: when one company (such as the **parent company** of a **media conglomerate**) owns a range of **media producers** or distribution networks across a variety of **media forms**. For example, the Disney group owns companies creating films, television programmes, video games and **magazines**.

- **Media synergy**: when two (or more) products help to promote each other, such as the video game or **music soundtrack** related to a film. The **release** of each product, and the engagement of the **audience**, helps to increase knowledge and sales of the other products.

Convergence can occur across different parts of the **media industry**, such as:

- **Content providers**: companies that create **media** products, or elements of **media** products, such as independent TV studios that create TV programmes for transmission on networks owned by other companies. **Convergence** of these companies can lead to less diversity of **media products**.

- **Network providers**: companies that broadcast, transmit or stream **media** products, such as Netflix, Amazon, Sky and ITV. **Convergence** of these companies can lead to consumers requiring fewer **subscriptions** to access more products, but also lack of access to some products that were more readily available.

- **Platform providers**: companies providing a **platform** for others to post their content, such as Facebook, YouTube and Vimeo. **Convergence** of these companies can lead to large businesses having greater access to consumers' data, offering more targeted choices based on a wider knowledge of the consumer.

The term '**platform**' can also be used to refer to the means of **transmission**, such as the internet, cable, satellite, terrestrial and DAB (for television and **radio** broadcasts), or to the **device** used to receive **media products**, such as a television set, **smartphone** or tablet. In the case of **devices** used to receive the **media**, **convergence** refers to the increasing ability to **consume** different **media** types on one **device**. For example, **smartphone users** can access the internet, television, **radio**, music, video games, films and digitised versions of print products on the same device.

The impact of **convergence** within the **media industry** is that there is an increasing **concentration of ownership**, with fewer companies controlling more of the available **media** products and markets, and the squeezing out of smaller, **independent companies**.

Knowledge Check 4.3

Explain how a **smartphone** enables you to access **digitally convergent** products, such as those created by the Bauer Kerrang! **brand**.

Funding and commercial industries 1

Spec Spotlight

The importance of different funding models. Government funded, not-for-profit and commercial models.

Role of:
- television licence
- advertising, sponsorship, product placement, direct sales
- independent and voluntary sector.

Media companies and **media** products are **funded** (or **financed**) in a variety of ways, with money coming directly from consumers, from **advertising** or from government funding and other grants.

Because of the methods of financing, companies can be labelled as:

- **Not-for-profit**: companies that don't take profits from their products and services.
- **Government funded**: companies receiving funds from the government of their country.
- **Commercial**: companies that make a profit for their owners or share-holders.
- Independent: not connected to the major companies.
- **Voluntary sector**: companies that are **non-profit** and non-governmental.

The BBC receives part of its income from the TV licence fee.

Income generation/revenue stream: these terms refer to the ways in which companies gather their **finance**, which include:

- **TV licence**: the BBC is partly **funded** by the **TV licence**, which has to be paid by most people in the UK who have equipment that can access BBC TV, including television sets, computers and gaming consoles. The **licence fee** is set and collected by the government, and passed on to the BBC.
- **Advertising**: other companies pay to place their adverts in or around **media** products. The income from these adverts **finances** the **media** company.
- **Sponsorship**: similar to **advertising**, a company pays to promote its **brand** in relation to a particular **media** product or aspect of a **media** product. For example, weather forecasts on **commercial** TV and **commercial radio** are often sponsored, and include the branding of their sponsor at the beginning and end.
- **Product placement**: deliberately using a branded product as a **prop** in a film, television show or video game, to promote that product through association with the **media product** and its characters. **Product placement** is paid for by the company selling the branded product.
- **Direct sales**: money is made by selling **media** products directly to the **audience**. This includes products such as DVDs, cinema ticket sales, **newspapers** and **magazines**.

  - **Subscription**: **newspapers**, **magazines** and video-on-demand services, among others, can often be paid for by **subscription** – a regular payment giving access to the products.
  - **Merchandise**: products such as games, toys, costumes, clothing, books and posters that are related to specific **media** output. **Direct sales** of these items can add to overall income, although some are **franchised** to other companies.

Netflix headquarters in Silicon Valley, Los Angeles

- **Freemium** games: these are free to play, but they have a **monetisation strategy** to enable them to be financially successful. This can include paid-for **in-app** or **in-game purchases**, **downloadable content (DLC)** and expansion packs for in-game **advertising**, and the ability to pay for a **premium** version of the game without adverts. Kim Kardashian: Hollywood is free to play, but players can pay for various upgrades or to gain prestige within the game.

- **Paymium** games: as **freemium** games, but there is a small upfront cost for the game. Lara Croft GO costs a small amount of money to play.

Through the **licence fee**, the BBC is a **publicly funded** organisation. In return for the **licence fee**, it is expected to provide a public service. It is therefore known as a **public service broadcaster (PSB)**. The BBC has a **charter** setting out what it must provide, and has a duty to inform, educate and entertain. It needs to provide a service for the whole population, across its output. The BBC is not allowed to carry **advertising** for other companies' products, but does create **merchandise** of its own, and sells its **media** products to other networks (usually abroad).

The TV channels that are on Freeview are **free-to-air**, while those that are broadcast specifically on Sky, Virgin Media and so on are paid for via **subscription**. Some TV programmes and films can be accessed online via one-off payments for specific content.

All the terrestrial **free-to-air** channels (BBC, ITV, Channel 4 and Channel 5) have a **public service remit**, giving them certain **responsibilities**, such as to cover the news and include arts and cultural programming.

Tip

Many **media** products are **financed** through a variety of methods. Be wary of over-generalising in an exam response. For example, it's not true to say 'The BBC receives its funding from the **licence fee**', but it is true to say 'The BBC receives part of its funding from the **licence fee**.'

Knowledge Check 4.4

Which of the terms used in this section can be applied to:
- the BBC?
- ITV?
- Sky?
- Netflix?

Funding and commercial industries 2

Spec Spotlight

How the media operate as commercial industries on a global scale and reach both large and specialised audiences.

- Globalisation.
- Cultural imperialism.
- International agreements (and disagreements) on regulation and freedom to trade media products.

Rapid Recap

Commercial industries

Commercial industries are industries that create and sell products and services for a profit.

Many **media** products target **audiences** within a given geographical area, so are **local**, **national** or global (worldwide) in outreach. Non-digital products tend to be distributed only in their relevant regions, e.g. the print version of a Coventry **local newspaper** can only be purchased in Coventry. The proliferation of digital products means that many more products are now available to a

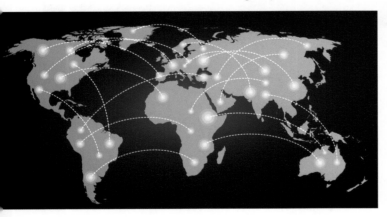

global audience even if they target a more **local audience**, e.g. Frome FM is a **local** community **radio** station centred around Frome in Somerset, but can be accessed via the internet from almost anywhere in the world.

This ability to distribute products globally has led to the ability to target large but specialised **audiences**. These are **niche audiences** in terms of being non-mainstream and loyal, but they are larger in scale than would otherwise have been possible because they can draw together individual fans from around the world.

Globalisation

Globalisation is the process of integrating and interacting with others around the world; and through this is the move towards a system of operations that is the same worldwide. For example, the '**globalisation** of the video games industry' refers to the ways in which video games companies operate around the world, drawing expertise from people in different countries, and **marketing** the same products to **audiences** around the globe.

The film and video games industries, along with the major TV **streaming services** such as Netflix and Amazon, are global in their outlook. Other **media** products are often more closely targeted at **local** or **national audiences**, but their originating companies may be located elsewhere in the world and sell to many different different countries around the world.

The concept and title of some **media** products are **franchised** to different countries, so that **local** versions can be made – for example, **reality TV** talent shows such as *The Voice* and *Strictly Come Dancing*, and TV comedy or drama series such as *The Office* and *House of Cards*.

Global companies, such as Disney, 21st Century Fox and Times Warner, can draw on their **finances** from **subsidiaries** and operations around the world to market any of their products as they try to attract new **audiences**. **Independent companies** have far fewer resources to draw on and therefore find it hard to compete.

Cultural imperialism

Cultural imperialism is the way in which cultural (including **media**) products and ideas from larger, more powerful nations, are exported into smaller, less powerful nations. This leads to a decrease in the **national** identity of the culture in those nations, as the imported culture starts to be seen as 'normal'. For example, the export of Hollywood films and American TV series around the globe means that apparent American **values** are shared via the **media**, even where they are at odds with **local** ones.

- Foreign imports: products brought into a country from other countries.
- Domestic products: products created within the country where they are being sold.
- Domestic market: the sales of goods created within a country, to consumers within the same country.

International agreements on regulation and trade

International agreements on **regulation** and trade are reached between governments about how to trade across **national** borders. In many cases taxes are imposed on foreign imports, making them more expensive to buy than domestic products. This is done to protect the domestic market, although it can cause a disagreement between nations. A major factor in the agreement to trade is the quality of **regulation** in the countries involved. For example, films shown in the UK must adhere to British laws and **regulations** concerning the use of animals and children, even if they are filmed in countries with different **regulations**.

Tip

Media One, Section B will include at least one 20-mark question. This will ask you to make judgements and draw conclusions. It will also ask you to use evidence from at least one of your CSPs (named in the question). It is possible that each of these aspects will be written into the marking criteria.

Knowledge Check 4.5

You are studying the following CSPs in relation to **Media Industries**. Note which are **targeting local**, **national** and **global audiences**.

Media form and CSP	Local, national or global?
Radio: Radio 1	
Radio: Beats 1 Radio	
Film: *Doctor Strange*	
Film: *I, Daniel Blake*	
Music video: Arctic Monkeys	
Music video: One Direction	
Television: *Doctor Who*	
Television: *Class*	
Newspapers: *Daily Mirror*	
Newspapers: *The Times*	
OSP media & video games: Zoella	
OSP media & video games: Kim Kardashian: Hollywood	
OSP media & video games: Lara Croft GO	

Production processes, job roles and working practices

Spec Spotlight

The impact of production processes, personnel and technologies on the final product.
Similarities and differences between media products in terms of when and where they are produced.
Working practices in media industries.

Rapid Recap

In **media industries**, the standard **production** process is to go through the stages of:

- **Production**: creating the product, which can be broken down into:
  - **pre-production** (research and planning)
  - **production** (e.g. filming for TV and film; writing **copy** and taking photographs for **magazines** and **newspapers**)
  - **post-production** (editing and finalising the product).
- Distribution: getting the product out to the **audience**, and **marketing** the product so that the **audience** want to engage with it.
- **Exhibition/exchange (sales)/consumption**: the means by which the **audience** can experience the product (e.g. watch on TV or video-on-demand, read the **magazine** or play the game).

People working in the **media industries** can be employed in a variety of ways. These include:

- **Salaried**: people receive regular payment (weekly or monthly) from their employer for the duration of their contract (temporary or permanent). Tax is deducted from their pay by their employers, and they have the right to holiday pay, maternity pay, parental leave, sick pay and redundancy pay. If the employer wants to end their contract early, the worker has to be made redundant or sacked because of proven misconduct.
- **Permanent contract**: no end date is set in the contract. The employee (worker) can choose to leave the job by giving a set period of notice.
- **Temporary contract/short-term contract**: an end date is set when the employee is first taken on. The contract could be for days, weeks or months. The employee could choose to leave before the end date, if a set period of notice is given.
- **Self-employed**: the worker is paid in full, without any deductions. They pay their own tax and national insurance, acting as their own **independent company**, working for the larger company that employs them. The worker is not paid holiday pay, etc. They are paid either for the specific period of time in which they work, or for a specific **project** to be completed.
- **Freelance**: **self-employed** workers who offer their services to organisations and take on work from a variety of sources.

A **freelance** video editor working on an independent **production**.

Job roles in the **media industries** can be roughly divided into **creative** and **non-creative roles**, including managerial, administrative and support roles.

- **Creative roles**: include **camera operator/photographer**, writer/**journalist**, designer, director and **editor**.
- Managerial, administrative and support roles: include **producer**, location manager, production assistant, finance and accounts, legal team, catering and transport.

Most creative workers in the **media industries** are **self-employed** and are taken on using **short-term contracts**. This enables employers to have a more flexible workforce, only paying each person for their specific contribution to a product.

On the film set of *Doctor Strange*

Filming *I, Daniel Blake*

The scale of a **media** product, the overall finance of the **production** company and the finance available to the product itself will determine how many people can be employed to work on that product. Small, **independent companies** such as Sixteen Films which produced *I, Daniel Blake* (**budget**: undisclosed, but includes grants from the BFI and BBC Films estimated at £2–3 million) will only be able to afford a much more compact **cast** and **crew** than larger, **multinational companies** such as Disney/Marvel who produced *Doctor Strange* (**budget**: $165,000,000).

IMDb lists a **cast** of 47 and a **crew** of 142 for *I, Daniel Blake*, and a **cast** of 77 and a **crew** of over 2,000 for *Doctor Strange*.

The **budget** for a **media** product will also affect the scale and scope of its **marketing**, with a higher **budget** enabling more paid-for **advertising**, across a wider geographical area. Due to the process of **vertical integration**, **media conglomerates** are able to distribute their own **media** products, whereas **independent film production** companies have to find a **distributor** and persuade them to take on their products.

Knowledge Check 4.6

Name at least three **creative roles** for each of the following industries:

- Film

1

2

3

- Newspapers

1

2

3

- Video games

1

2

3

Tip

Some of the pairs of CSPs have contrasting **Media Industry** contexts, for example the two **music** videos and the two films. In these cases, if you are asked about the impact of the industry on **media** products, a comparison between the two CSPs would be a useful approach you could take.

Regulation

Links

For more on regulation see pages 128–132, 143–144 and 147–148 of the student book

Spec Spotlight

The functions and types of regulation of the media.

Self-regulation and government regulation.

Disputes about freedom, censorship and control.

Nature of regulatory bodies in UK:

- the Office of Communications (OFCOM)
- the Independent Press Standards Organisation (IPSO)
- the Video Standards Council (VSC)
- the British Board of Film Classification (BBFC)
- the Advertising Standards Authority (ASA)
- Pan European Game Information (PEGI).

Rapid Recap

- **Regulation**: the majority of **media industries** are regulated, setting rules they have to abide by, to protect the public, consumers and citizens. **Regulation** attempts to protect people from potentially harmful or unsuitable material, to prevent harm to people (and animals) during the **production** process, and to empower people to make informed decisions about what they choose to watch, listen to or read.

- **Statutory regulation**: statutory **regulators** have legal powers to control the industry they are responsible for. They set and enforce the rules for these industries.

- **Government regulation**: some **media industries** are **regulated** by government-controlled organisations. These include the television and **radio** industries.

- **Self-regulation**: some **media industries** set up and pay for their own organisations to regulate their industries. These include the **newspaper** and film industries. These **regulatory bodies** do not have legal powers, but agree and advise on a code of practice.

- **Ofcom**: the Office of Communications is the **government-funded regulator** for the TV, **radio** and telecommunications industries in the UK.

- **IPSO**: the Independent Press Standards Organisation regulates the **newspaper** industry in the UK, along with **IMPRESS**, which is the government's preferred **regulator** but is not recognised by most **national newspapers**. IPSO is a **self-regulatory** body, whereas **IMPRESS** is independent of the major **newspapers**.

- **VSC**: the Video Standards Council operates the **PEGI age rating** system in the UK.

bbfc View what's right for you

The British Board of Film Classification is an **independent**, non-governmental body that classifies films and videos in the UK.

Campaigning march for press freedom in Istanbul. Many Turkish **journalists** have been jailed for criticising the regime.

- **BBFC**: the British Board of Film Classification regulates the film industry in the UK, by giving advisory **age ratings** to films. The **BBFC** is a **self-regulatory** body, which was set up in 1913.
- **ASA**: the Advertising Standards Authority regulates the **advertising** industry in the UK.
- **PEGI**: Pan European Game Information regulates the video game industry across Europe, including the UK, by setting **age ratings** for games.
- **IPSO** and **IMPRESS**: were set up in 2014 after the Leveson Enquiry into the 'phone hacking scandal' at News International from 2005 to 2011, particularly focusing on the *News of the World*, which concluded that the previous **regulatory body**, the Press Complaints Commission, was ineffective. As a result of the scandal, several **journalists** received prison sentences, and the *News of the World* paid compensation to some of the victims.
- The **public interest**: this is not the same as 'of interest to the public'. It refers to information that the public should know for their own safety, security and wellbeing. Sharing information about a major chemical spill is in the **public interest**, whereas sharing information about a celebrity fall-out is simply interesting to some members of the public.

Press regulation has to balance the **freedom of the press** with the rights of individuals. The **freedom of the press** allows **journalists** to investigate controversial stories, and express opinions critical of the government. Individual people have a right to live their private lives without harassment or intrusion by the press.

Some **media regulators** set **age classifications** for products in their relevant industry, such as **BBFC** and **PEGI**. These are guidelines for others to enforce.

Ofcom's Broadcasting Code states that programmes, **trailers** and adverts which are not suitable for children should not be shown between 9pm and 5.30am – 9pm is referred to as the **watershed**. **Paid-for services** such as Sky Movies are not required to abide by the **watershed**, but must be protected by a password or PIN.

FREE MEDIA CANNOT BE SILENCED

FREE MEDIA PLATFORM

Knowledge Check 4.7

Match the **regulatory body** to the **media industry**.

Regulatory body	Media industry
Ofcom	Newspapers
BBFC	Television
IPSO	Film
ASA	Video games
IMPRESS	Newspapers and magazines
PEGI	Advertising
VSC	Video games

Tip

Media Two will end with a **synoptic question**, in which you are expected to draw together knowledge and understanding from across the full course of study. In this question, you could, for example, be asked to link the ownership of a **media industry** with the **media language** and **media representations** used in particular products.

Digital technologies and media regulation

Spec Spotlight

The challenges for media regulation presented by 'new' digital technologies.
Debates about:
* online, social networking abuse and bullying
* online anonymity
* rights and responsibilities of ISPs and social networks
* public interest versus rights of the individual.

Rapid Recap

* 'New' digital technologies: internet-based technologies that allow access by **audiences** around the world, as well as **audience interaction** and the **uploading** of user-generated content (UGC). These include **social networks, websites** and **online gaming**.

* **Social networks**: links between people created via internet-based **social media** apps and sites, such as Facebook, Twitter, Instagram, Snapchat and YouTube. Many allow their **users** to remain **anonymous** by **selecting user-names**. **Users** are also able to set up **fake accounts** in other people's names. **Online anonymity** allows people to behave differently online, including:

Cyber-bullying by text

- **Cyber-bullying**: bullying of individuals via mobile phones and **social networks**.
- **Trolling**: deliberately starting quarrels and upsetting people online by adding controversial comments to **social media** feeds.
- **Flaming**: posting insults and personal attacks on **social networks**.

- **ISPs**: **internet service providers** are the companies that provide the means to access the **internet**, including connecting **devices** to **websites**, email and online storage. All **devices** that are connected online must be routed through an **ISP**. The **ISP** keeps an electronic trace of all online activity, both **uploading** and **downloading** information. **ISPs** includes companies such as BT, Sky Broadband, Virgin Media and TalkTalk.

- **Social networks** and **websites** are not subject to **external regulatory bodies**, and, as they are available across international borders, they are hard to govern through **national** laws. Most **social networks** have conditions their **users** must agree to. These are listed under titles such as: Terms of Service, Community Standards, User Agreements or Community Rules. **Social networks** distance themselves from the content posted on their **platforms** by **users**; they usually rely on other **users** to report offensive content, which is then checked and can be removed if it is deemed to have broken the network's rules. There is ongoing **controversy** over whether **social networks** are also **publishers**, which would give them more **responsibility** over what is posted on their **platforms**.

- **ISPs** also distance themselves from the content posted via their services, including complete **websites**. **ISPs** can be prosecuted for allowing the posting of indecent and offensive material that breaks the laws of a given nation. They will usually remove the offending sites to avoid prosecution. Some **website** owners deliberately host their sites with a number of **ISPs** to avoid being taken down.

- **Public interest**: events, **issues** or concerns that affect the wellbeing of the general public.

- **Individual rights**: each person has rights decided by the country or community they live in, as well as the Universal Declaration of Human Rights. These rights usually include a right to privacy and a right to live without harassment.

- There is a **conflict** between **public interest** and **individual rights** if, for example, protecting our data online allows anonymous people to intentionally harm others.

Knowledge Check 4.8

Sort these companies into **ISPs** and **social media networks**.

Company	ISP	Social media network
Facebook		
Virgin Media		
BT		
EE		
Snapchat		
Twitter		
Flickr		
Sky Broadband		
Talk Talk		
Instagram		
Vodafone		
YouTube		

Tip

Media Two will assess your understanding and knowledge of the in-depth CSPs, covering **television**, **newspapers**, **online, social and participatory media** and **video games**. You could be asked about the theoretical framework area of **Media Industries** in relation to any of these.

Check It

1 Define the term 'conglomerate'.

2 What is the difference between a merger and a demerger?

3 Give an example of vertical integration.

4 Give an example of horizontal integration.

5 Explain one advantage and one disadvantage of concentration of ownership.

6 What is the difference between an independent company and a subsidiary?

7 Define the term 'diversification'.

8 What does the intellectual property of a film company refer to?

9 What is digital convergence?

10 Give an example of a company involved in cross-media ownership.

11 List three ways in which a commercial media company can be financed.

12 Who sets the rate for the TV licence fee, and who does the money go to?

13 How can a freemium video game make money?

14 What is a public service broadcaster?

15 Explain what 'globalisation' means.

16 What does 'cultural imperialism' refer to?

(Continued on the next page)

17 What are the three major stages of the media industry process?

18 Name at least three managerial, administrative or support jobs in the media industries.

19 What is the difference between a salaried and a self-employed worker?

20 What is the purpose of regulation in the media?

21 Define the term 'self-regulation'.

22 Which organisation regulates the film industry in the UK?

23 What does PEGI stand for?

24 What is the role of IPSO?

25 What is the watershed on TV?

26 What does ISP stand for?

27 Explain the term 'the public interest'.

28 Name three social media networks.

29 Why is the internet difficult to regulate?

30 What is 'trolling'?

5 Media Audiences

Spec Spotlight

How the media forms target, reach and address audiences, how audiences interpret and respond to them, and how members of the audience become producers themselves.

Audience theories and audience interpretations 1

Spec Spotlight

Theoretical perspectives on audiences including:
- active and passive audiences
- audience response
- audience interpretation.

Rapid Recap

Audiences are said to **consume** the **media**. They are **media consumers**, and we study their patterns of **consumption**.

Theories about the effects of the **media** on the **audience**, or vice versa, make assumptions about whether the **audience** is active or passive.

Passive audiences

- **Passive audiences**: the **audiences** choose which **media** to **consume**, but then simply soak up the **media** output they have chosen. They accept the **media**'s messages.
- **Effects theory**: claims that the **media** have a direct influence on the attitudes and behaviour of both individuals and society.
- **Hypodermic needle theory**/hypodermic syringe theory: this is a theory from the 1930s; the **media** directly injects its messages into the **audience**, in the same way that a drug user may inject harmful drugs, creating a uniform **response**. The **audience** cannot escape from the **media**'s influence. Used to explain the response to Nazi **propaganda** and other **media** messages.

Link

For more on **passive audiences** see page 97 of the student book.

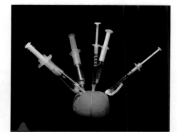

The **media** have been likened to hypodermic needles.

Tip

You are studying the following **media forms** in relation to **Media Audiences**: radio, music video, television, newspapers, online, social and participatory media and video games. You could be asked about any of these, with the exception of television, in Media One Section B. There may also be questions related to **Media Audiences** in Media Two.

Link

For more on **active audiences** see pages 97–100 of the student book.

- **Cultivation theory**: long-term exposure to **media** messages gives the **audience** a distorted view of society, so people think it is more violent and less safe than their experience of real life would suggest.
- **Desensitisation**: **audiences** exposed to frequent violent **images** in the **media** (e.g. through video games) respond with less sympathy to real-life violence and tragedy.

Knowledge Check 5.1

Does the **hypodermic needle theory** assume that the **audience** is active or passive?

Audience theories and audience interpretations 2

Spec Spotlight

Theoretical perspectives on audiences including:

- active and passive audiences
- audience response
- audience interpretation.

Blumler and Katz's uses and gratifications theory.

The role of audiences in the creation of meaning and the degree of effect of media messages upon audiences.

Rapid Recap

Active audiences and audience response

Active audiences: the **audience** chooses to use the **media** for a variety of different reasons, and chooses how to understand the **media** by making their own **meanings** from the coded information in it. They can challenge the **media**'s messages.

Blumler and Katz's uses and gratifications theory (or model): **audience** members actively seek out specific **media products** to meet their individual needs at that time. People use the **media** to provide gratifications for their needs.

The major needs are defined as:

- **Entertainment and diversion**: wanting to relax and escape from everyday lives.
- Information and education (also called **surveillance**): finding out about the real world.

Watching television for **entertainment** and **social interaction**.

- **Social interaction**: allowing people to be part of a community, either interacting with other **audience** members by talking about the **media product** (face-to-face or online), or regarding the characters and personalities in the **media** as friends/companions.
- **Personal identity**: comparing ourselves to, or measuring ourselves against, role models in the **media**.

Other pleasures provided by the **media** include:

- **Aesthetic pleasure**: appreciating beauty.
- **Cerebral pleasure**: enjoying using the brain, solving an intellectual challenge.
- **Visceral pleasure**: feeling something in an almost physical way, such as 'stomach-churning' or 'heart-pounding'.
- **Voyeuristic pleasure**: enjoying spying on others.
- **Vicarious pleasure**: enjoying experiences second-hand by watching others go through them.
- **Catharsis**: getting rid of pent-up emotions.

Two-step flow is when **audience** members' reaction to the **media** is partly influenced by the reactions of their family, friends and other role models.

Moral panic is an extreme **audience response**.

Link

For more on **audience** pleasure see page 100 of the student book.

Link

See Chapter 3 page 75 of this book for more on **moral panic**.

Knowledge Check 5.2

Match the term to its description.

Use for/pleasure in the media	Description
Diversion	Finding out about the world.
Aesthetic pleasure	Being part of a community.
Information/surveillance	Wanting to relax and escape everyday life.
Cerebral pleasure	Getting rid of frustrations.
Social interaction	Enjoying beautiful things.
Catharsis	Comparing oneself to others.
Personal identity	Spying on other people.
Voyeuristic pleasure	Solving intellectual challenges.

Playing video games can be very **cathartic**.

Tip

Blumler and Katz are **media theorists** who are named in the specification, so you could be asked a direct question about their **uses and gratifications theory**. The **narrative** theorist **Propp** is also mentioned by name. Other theorists are not named, so you will not be asked directly about them, but you could apply other theories you know where they are relevant to a question.

Audience theories and audience interpretations 3

Spec Spotlight

The ways in which audiences may interpret the same media products very differently and how these differences may reflect both social and individual differences.

- Reception theories.
- Active audiences.
- Preferred and aberrant readings.

Active audiences.

Influence of social variables on audience perception.

How audiences may respond to and interpret media products.

Why these responses and interpretations may change over time.

Rapid Recap

Link

For more on categorising different **audience segments** see page 115 of this book.

One Direction perform 'History' in their 2016 music video.

Each member of the **audience** brings their own experiences to bear on any **media product** they **consume**. They all have a **situated culture** – the environment they were brought up in, including their friends, family and wider community. They also have a **mediated culture** – the ideas and experiences they have been exposed to because of the **media products** they have **consumed**. These different cultures affect how each person **interprets** and reacts to a **media product**.

For example, a 20-year-old female pop music fan, who has grown up with the **music** of One Direction, will interpret the 'History' video differently from a 15-year-old male grime fan.

Stuart Hall's **reception theory** explores how different **audience** members may interpret the same **media product**.

Media producers encode their **meanings** into the product, using **signs**. **Media audiences** decode the **meanings** by reading these **signs**. However, if the **producer** and **audience** don't share common experiences and a **common culture** then the **meanings** may be interpreted differently. **Media** products are **polysemic** – they can convey a number of **meanings**.

Reception theory suggests three different ways an **audience** might decode these intended **meanings**:

- **Preferred reading**: understanding and accepting the producer's intended **meanings**.
- **Negotiated reading**: accepting some of the intended **meanings** and rejecting others.
- **Oppositional reading**: recognising the **preferred reading** but rejecting it.

Link

For more on **reception theories** see pages 100–102 of the student book.

A potential fourth decoding is the:

- **Aberrant reading**: misunderstanding the **meanings** and **superimposing** others because of a difference in cultural understanding.

Audience positioning

Media producers use a range of techniques to steer the **audience** towards the **preferred reading**; they try to control the reaction or **position** of the **audience**. One of these techniques is to adopt a specific **mode of address** (the manner in which the product 'talks' to the **audience**). For example, **media language** may be used to make the product seem authoritative, to **position** the **audience** as learning from the product. Or it may be made to seem 'matey', to **position** the **audience** as being a friend. In both cases, this makes the **media product** feel harder to doubt or reject.

The wider the differences in **social variables** (**age**, gender, **social class**, ethnicity) between the producers' intended **audience** and the actual **audience**, the less likely the **audience** are to accept the **preferred reading**.

As social culture changes with time, so do **readings** of **media products**. Susan, in the first episode of *Doctor Who*, was seen as being a hyper-intelligent version of a normal teenager by the **audience** of the time. For both 1960s and current **audiences** she is a mysterious character with exceptional unexplained scientific knowledge, but her accent and the different way she addresses women from men would now be seen as outdated.

Audiences can be said to be active in several different ways:

- They select **media products** for their own **uses and gratifications**.
- They interpret **media products** through their own decoding, rather than necessarily accepting the meaning encoded by the **media producer**.
- Particularly through digital **media**, they can create products themselves that could potentially reach a **mass audience**, e.g. through YouTube. This can include fan-made products related to the **media** they are consuming, such as **fan-made trailers** for major film **releases**.
- Again through digital **media**, they can **interact** with the producers of **mass media products**.

Link

For more on **audience positioning** see pages 102–104 of the student book.

Link

See the discussion of **audience variables** on page 108 of this book.

The character of Susan from *Doctor Who*'s 'An Unearthly Child' no longer seems anything like a normal teenager.

Tip

You could be asked how **media products** address their **audiences**. In a question like this, you would be pointed towards specific **media** products such as the two **newspaper** CSPs. It could be helpful to contrast two products within the same **media form**, to point out the differences between them.

Knowledge Check 5.3

Which of these is the **preferred reading**, which is the **oppositional reading** and which is the **negotiated reading** of Kim Kardashian: Hollywood?

		Reading
a	The celebrity lifestyle is glamorous and fun but shallow.	
b	Fame and success can be achieved by anyone if they try hard enough.	
c	Hollywood celebrities are self-centred and obsessed with material wealth.	

Categorising audiences

Spec Spotlight

How media organisations categorise audiences.
Segmentation and variables:

- geographic
- demographic
- psychographic.

Rapid Recap

The proliferation of **media** channels and products, especially since the advent of digital **media**, has led to **fragmentation** of the **audience**, as each **media product** attracts a smaller proportion of the overall **market share**.

The first episode of *Doctor Who* in 1963, when there were only two television channels in the UK, gained 4.4 million viewers. Approximately 2 million of the 11 million households in the UK that had a television were tuned in to the episode.

The fourth episode of *Class* gained just over 0.3 million viewers when it was shown on BBC One, and almost 0.6 million in total when the online viewers on BBC Three were added.

When defining **audiences** for a product, **media industries** use **audience segmentation** – ways to break down the **audience** into distinct groups or segments. Each segment of the **audience** is defined by something they have in common, such as their **age** group.

Key methods of **segmentation** include:

- **Geographic**: where the **audience** is based. For example, the *Daily Mirror* targets a UK-based **audience**.

- **Demographic**: information about statistical **audience variables**, including gender, **social class**, ethnicity, **age** and generation. The word comes from *demos* meaning people, and *graphy* meaning written or drawn representation. For example, *Class* targets an older teenage **audience**.

- **Psychographic**: information about the **audience variables** of values, attitudes, opinions and lifestyles. The word comes from *psycho* meaning the mind and *graphy* meaning written or drawn representation. For example, Zoella targets an **audience** interested in make-up and fashion.

The most well-known of the **demographic** classification systems is the **NRS socio-economic scale**, devised by the National Readership Survey.

Audience ratings for each episode of *Class*.

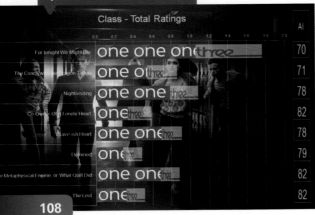

Class - Total Ratings		AI
For tonight We Might Die	one one one three	70
The Coach with the Dragon Tattoo	one o three	71
Nightvisiting	one one three	78
Co-Owner of a Lonely Heart	one three	82
Brave-ish Heart	one one three	78
Detained	one three	79
the Metaphysical Engine, or What Quill Did	one one three	82
The Lost	one three	82

Grade	Description	% of UK population in 2017
A	Higher managerial, administrative and professional	5
B	Intermediate managerial, administrative and professional	23
C1	Supervisory, clerical and junior managerial, administrative and professional	23
C2	Skilled manual workers	20
D	Semi-skilled and unskilled manual workers	15
E	State pensioners, casual and lowest grade workers, unemployed with state benefits only	9

Source: National Readership Survey, 2018

Some of the models for categorising or classifying **audiences** using **psychographics** include Young & Rubicam's 4 Cs (Cross Cultural Consumer Characteristics), VALS™ (Values, Attitudes and Lifestyles Survey) and Experian's Mosaic. Each of these has been developed to enable **marketing companies** to target their **audiences** more accurately.

Using **geographic**, **demographic** and **psychographic** information, an **audience profile** can be built up.

Knowledge Check 5.4

Using **geographic**, **demographic** and **psychographic** information, define the **target audiences** for Beats 1 Radio, Radio 1, *Doctor Who* and *Class*.

Tip

Your teacher may have taught you any one of the **psychographic** models mentioned above, or may have used a different **psychographic** classification model. There is no one method that is better than another, and you don't need to know them all, as they all are different ways of approaching the same information. You can discuss **audience profiles** and **audience profiling**, using whatever method you have been taught.

Targeting a range of audiences 1

Spec Spotlight

How and why media products are aimed at a range of audiences, from small, specialised audiences to large mass audiences.

Requirement for commercial media producers to create audiences which can be sold to advertisers.

Rapid Recap

- **Mass audience**: a very large **audience**, usually of millions of people.
- **Niche audience**: a smaller, more specialised **audience**. One meaning of the word 'niche' is a small slot in a wall, in which something can be placed. Think of a **niche audience** as occupying a small slot in the **media** landscape. A product aimed at a **niche audience** will fit this slot perfectly, **targeting** the needs of that specific group of people. Because the products fit so well, the **niche audience** tends to be very loyal. For example, Freesports TV offers live coverage of ice hockey matches, which have a **niche audience** in the UK but a **mass audience** in the USA and Canada.

Because it is specialised, a **niche audience** will include a smaller proportion of the population than a **mass audience**. However, if this is an international **audience**, it could still be very large in size.

Media producers need to know their product has an **audience** for one of the following reasons:

- They need the **audience** to buy (pay for) the product – **direct sales**.
- They need good **audience** numbers to justify a **subsidy** or other financial support (e.g. television **licence fees**).
- They need to sell **advertising** space, and **advertisers** will only pay to reach the right **audience**.

Media companies that make money from **direct sales** and/or **advertising** are **commercial** companies, creating products to make a profit for their owners or shareholders.

Some **media** commentators have said that **media products** are created to sell **audiences** to **advertisers**. In 2010, a comment on the Metafilter website by blue_beetle said:

If you are not paying for it, you're not the customer; you're the product being sold. (cited at https://quoteinvestigator.com/2017/07/16/product/)

Tip ✓

Be prepared to define terms such as **mainstream**, **mass** or **niche audience**, and **psychographics** or **demographics**.

Television channels sell their **audiences** to their advertisers.

Advertisers want their adverts to be seen by the target market for their products and services, so are interested in knowing exactly who the **audience** is composed of for each **media product**, such as each specific TV programme, **magazine** or website. **Commercial media** companies share the **demographic** and **psychographic** information about their **audiences** with potential **advertisers**, to entice them to pay for **advertising**.

Knowledge Check 5.5

Sort these **media products** into two lists, those aimed at **mainstream audiences** and those aimed at **niche audiences**.

Mainstream audiences	Niche audiences

- *Daily Mirror*
- *Doctor Who*
- *Class*
- *Farmers Weekly* magazine
- *15 Minute Drama* on Radio 4
- Lara Croft GO
- One Direction – 'History' music video
- Korpiklaani – 'A Man with a Plan' music video (Finnish folk metal band)
- Instagram
- NHS Blood and Transplant campaign video, 'Represent featuring Lady Leshurr'

Targeting a range of audiences 2

Spec Spotlight

The ways in which media organisations target audiences through marketing.

Understanding of the assumptions organisations make about their target audience(s).

Role of genre conventions in the targeting of audiences.

Techniques used in the marketing of media products:
- guerrilla and viral marketing
- trailers, tasters and teasers.

Rapid Recap

To attract **media audiences**, producers must **market** their products, ensuring that the **target audience** are aware the product exists and know how to access it. They define their **target audience** using **demographic** and **psychographic variables**. For example, the original **target audience** of Radio 1, when it was launched in 1967, was young people aged 15–29, particularly those who were likely to listen to existing **pirate radio stations**.

Media producers like to create products within existing **genres** because they can market these to existing **audiences** who already enjoy the **genre**. They often emphasise **conventions** from the **genre** in their **marketing** to persuade the **audience** that the product will feel familiar and therefore be enjoyable.

Media producers and **distributors** use a range of methods to market their products. **Marketing** encompasses more than **paid-for advertising**, including **interviews**, publicity stunts, poster campaigns and other outdoor **advertising**, DVD and video game covers, and merchandise as well as the following methods:

- **Viral marketing**: **marketing** that encourages and relies on the sharing of information, video files and so on from one person to another via **social networks**; similar to the spreading of a virus from one person to another in the real world.

- **Guerrilla marketing**: unconventional **marketing** ideas that are low cost, and that promote products in public places. This includes events such as flashmobs and installations such as the (fake) 'Persona Synthetics' shop-front in London, which was used to market Channel 4's TV drama series *Humans*. The **audience** should engage with a surprising and memorable experience which they will share by word of mouth, including **social media**. Guerrilla marketers hope that the online sharing of their posts and stunts will 'go viral'.

- A campaign or video is said to **go viral** when it reaches a high number of people over **social networks** within a relatively short time, for example over five million views within a three- to seven-day period.

- **Non-linear marketing**: **marketing** that encourages the **audience** to take action (often online or on **social media**) *before* getting to the real point of the campaign, investing time and emotion in the product before they know what it is. For example, the 'Persona Synthetics'/*Humans* **marketing** shown on the right carried the **hashtag** '#Humans' but no mention of television or Channel 4. The **audience** shared and commented on what they had seen before checking on the **hashtag** and finding **links** to the show's own web presence.

- **Trailers**: originally **commercial** adverts for forthcoming films, to be shown in cinemas. At first, they were shown after the main film, *trailing* it. Obviously, cinemas now show them before films. The term **trailer** also now includes similar **advertising** for television shows, video games, theatre events and concerts.

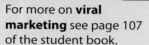

Link

For more on **viral marketing** see page 107 of the student book.

Link

For more on **guerrilla marketing** and **advertising** see page 188 of the student book.

This shop-front for fake store 'Persona Synthetics' was part of a wider **guerrilla marketing** campaign for Channel 4's *Humans*.

Closer to humans than ever before

- **Tasters**: a sample or preview of a product, for example Artic Monkey's 'I Bet You Look Good on the Dancefloor' **music video** acted as a **taster** for their first album, *Whatever People Say I Am, That's What I'm Not*.

- **Teasers**: **marketing** that is meant to intrigue the **audience**, arousing their curiosity. In the film industry, **teaser trailers** or film **teasers** are **released** long before the film is due out, with far less content than a **trailer**, and usually carry a general release date such as 'next summer'. Apparent leaks of information on **social media** about forthcoming **media products** could also be regarded as **teasers**.

Doctor Strange, like most Marvel films, contained two **teaser scenes** (or **stingers**) in the credits, pointing towards the next movies in the *Avengers* **franchise**.

Mid-credits **teaser scene** from *Doctor Strange*

 Knowledge Check 5.6

How did the NHS Blood and Transplant advert and the Galaxy 'Audrey Hepburn' advert use the conventions of specific **genres** to target their intended **audiences**?

 Tip

Bear in mind that *you* are not always within the **target audience** for a specific **media** product, and therefore you cannot assume that your personal views about the product reflect those of the intended **audience**. Look for evidence in the product and its **marketing** to work out who that **audience** is or was.

Technologies and measuring audiences

Spec Spotlight

The role of media technologies in reaching and identifying audiences, and in audience consumption and usage.

Use of online resources to collect audience data.

Audience research institutions including the Broadcasters Audience Research Board (BARB), Radio Joint Audience Research Limited (RAJAR), Pamco, Nielsen.

Research techniques:

- quantitative/qualitative
- primary/secondary.

Link

For more on audience research see page 93 of the student book.

Link

For more on **psychographics** see page 161 of the student book.

Audience research institutions, such as BARB, gather statistics about the way people use the media.

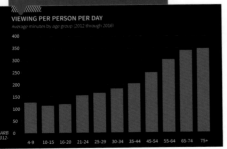

VIEWING PER PERSON PER DAY
Average minutes by age group (2012 through 2016)

Source: BARB Panel – 2012-2016

Rapid Recap

Audience research is carried out to provide **audience** data – information about the **demographics** and **psychographics** of the **audiences** for specific **media products**.

This information is mainly used to attract **advertisers** to pay for **advertising** space. **Psychographics** are important in telling **advertisers** about the **audience**'s priorities for their leisure time and for spending their money.

The audience research organisations include:

- **ABC**: Audit Bureau of Circulations, gathers and verifies data about print and digital media. It looks specifically at the number of copies of print **media** in circulation and the **audience** reach of websites.
- **BARB**: Broadcasters Audience Research Board, who gather data about television viewing, including time-shift viewing. This is viewing a scheduled programme after the scheduled slot, using home recording technologies or online catch-up.
- **Nielsen**: a data analytics company that combines its own data collection with data from a range of sources, to provide information about the **audiences** for different **media forms**.
- **PAMCo**: Publishers Audience Measurement Company. This organisation took over from the NRS (National Readership Survey) in gathering data about **newspaper** and **magazine audiences**, both in print form and online.
- **RAJAR**: Radio Joint Audience Research, jointly owned by the BBC and commercial **radio** services, who gather data about **radio** listeners.

Most of these organisations are independent of the industries for whom they measure the **audiences**, even though they receive **funding** from those industries. This is because they are supplying figures to **advertisers** who need to be able to trust them.

Research methods

- **Quantitative research**: is about statistics and numbers. Questions are factual and closed, with a small range of potential answers. The data provided are statistical, for example the number of people who read *The Times* each day, or the proportion of readers who are aged under 35.

- **Qualitative research**: is about opinions and attitudes. Questions are more open-ended. The information provided is about **psychographics**, for example that readers of *The Times* like to read about education and, as they are regular visitors to the cinema, also films.

- **Primary research**: research 'from scratch', where the organisation is carrying out the initial research themselves. **BARB** use devices attached to the televisions of volunteer families to carry out **primary research** into what those families watch. **Primary research** methods include:

  - **focus groups**: a group of people brought together to discuss an issue, product or campaign, in order for a researcher to collect information about their opinions

  - questionnaires

  - interviews

  - surveys.

- **Secondary research**: when an organisation is finding out what other people have already discovered about a given subject. **Nielsen** combines some of the research from other organisations to work out a broader picture of a given **audience segment**'s **media** habits.

The nature of data collection has changed as **digital platforms** have become more prevalent even *within* **traditional media industries** such as **newspapers**, **radio** and **television**.

BARB has a panel of 5,300 households at any one time, each of which has **devices** fitted to their televisions, PCs and tablets to measure scheduled TV and **BVOD** (broadcaster video on demand) viewing. The people in these households sign in and out on the **device** as they enter and leave the room it is in.

BARB device, monitoring what is shown on a TV set.

This information is combined with data that come direct from **BVOD** devices (computers, tablets and **smartphones**) across the country, showing how many **devices** are logged into each service and what is being viewed. Having both sets of data allows **BARB** to work out how many *people*, and which **audience segments**, are watching each TV programme within a seven-day period.

PAMCo combines the data from 35,000 face-to-face interviews each year with the data from 5,000 participants who have agreed to have a Tracker App installed on their **digital devices**. Combining these data sets enables **PAMCo** to understand whether people are accessing the same publications in both print and online versions.

RAJAR uses a weekly sample of approximately 2,000 people, both adults and children, across every **radio** station's geographical areas. Each person selected has a self-completion diary for seven days, either paper-based or online. The diary is divided into 15-minute segments.

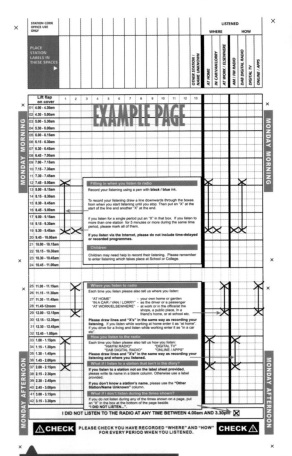

RAJAR diary sample page

Knowledge Check 5.7

Note whether each of these statements is true or false:

1. **PAMCo** measures the **audience** size in the **newspaper** industry.

2. **BARB** carries out interviews with householders to find out what they have watched on TV.

3. **Nielsen** uses data from other organisations to create an overview of different **media audiences**.

4. **RAJAR** uses surveys to find out about the **psychographics** of the **radio audience**.

Tip ✓

You will not be directly asked for specific facts about **audiences** or industries, such as the number of readers of the *Daily Mirror*. However, this sort of information could be useful to bring into a longer response question, as evidence to back up a point you are making.

Social, historical, political and cultural contexts

Spec Spotlight

The social, cultural and political significance of media products:
- the themes or issues they address
- the fulfilment of needs and desires
- the functions they serve in society and everyday life.

Rapid Recap

Media products are created at a particular time and place with a particular community in mind. **Media producers** select and design their content in order to create products that **audiences** will engage with.

These products therefore fit into the cultural, social and media landscapes of their time, either echoing or **subverting** the **themes** and **issues** seen in other **media** and cultural products. **Media producers** often pick up on **themes** and **issues** being debated in society and amplify these within their products, making the **audience** more likely to watch, listen or read to find out more.

For example, the film *I, Daniel Blake* explores the **issues** of austerity and the benefit system: controversial topics since the introduction of austerity measures in 2008.

The television series *Doctor Who* was launched between the first successful manned space flight (April 1961) and the first moon landing (July 1969), in a period when the major world powers were competing to make this happen. Its science fiction theme tapped into the issue of space travel.

Doctor Who could also be seen as fulfilling the **desires** of the **audience**, as it gave fictional answers to their questions, hopes and fears about what was 'out there'.

Another way in which **media producers** try to fulfil the **audience**'s needs and **desires** is by providing **media** products that are similar to those the **audience** has recently enjoyed – within the same **genre**, the same **media form** or the same **brand** or **franchise**. When they created Lara Croft GO, Square Enix combined the Tomb Raider **franchise** with the puzzle-based game **genre** of Hitman GO.

Lara Croft GO is sold alongside Hitman GO and Deus Ex GO, all developed by Square Enix.

Tip ✓

The **synoptic question** at the end of Media Two will ask you to draw together your knowledge of the different areas of the theoretical framework and the **media contexts**. This could include the **significance** (cultural, social, historical or political) of the specific **media products** named in the question.

The **function** of many **media** products for the **audience** is to provide entertainment. This is true of video games such as Kim Kardashian: Hollywood, a **casual role-playing game** that can be played by its **audience** in short bursts, wherever they are. However, in common with many **media products**, it also serves the function of reflecting back to the **audience** the **values** and goals of contemporary society.

Other functions of **media** products include:

● Setting the **political agenda** (e.g. *The Times*).

● Commenting on society (e.g. *I, Daniel Blake*).

● Enabling the **audience** to come together to discuss the same topics (e.g. **social media**).

Knowledge Check 5.8

How does each of these products reflect the **values** and goals of contemporary society: Beats 1 Radio, Zoella's vlog posts, *Class* and the *Daily Mirror*? Do the particular editions you have studied pick up on any **themes** or **issues** in society?

Audience's media practices and audience responses

Spec Spotlight

The ways in which people's media practices are connected to their identity, including their sense of actual and desired self.

Identity and audience membership.

Fans and fandom.

Talking about the media.

How audiences may respond to and interpret media products and why these responses and interpretations may change over time.

How changing cultural values with reference to, for example, gender roles, ethnic identities have influenced contemporary perceptions of historical products.

Rapid Recap

People's **media** practices include the ways they **consume** the **media**, **interact** with the **media** and create **media** products themselves.

Audience members can create their own **media identity**, especially using online resources and **user-generated content**. Because of the potential for anonymity, people can choose to *re-create* themselves with new identities. Some of the methods they can use to do this online include:

- **Blogs**: weblogs; websites or pages in the form of personal online journals that are updated regularly. Bloggers can mediate their life concentrating on their ideas and successes in a specialist area.

- **Citizen journalism**: anyone can send photographs or text from their mobile phone to news agencies, **newspapers** or news broadcasters. These often add to the overall picture of a story.

- **Comments**: most comments on websites are posted using user names that hide the true identity of the person posting and allow them to take on a new identity.

- **Content sharing**: using **social media**, people can send **links** for web content to each other, boosting their own **profile** and giving a specific impression of themselves as they do so.

- **Crowd sourcing**: there is an array of online sites seeking the ideas, opinions, services, funds and signatures of large numbers of people to help push **projects** forward.

- **Livestreaming**: broadcasting the live view from a mobile phone via **social media** and other apps.

CROWD
SOURCING

- **Podcasts**: audio-only episodes posted online, many are like audio **blogs**, with regular subscribers listening to the latest updates.
- **Social media profiles**: people can choose their own **images** and post content, creating their own **narrative** of their life.
- **Vlogs**: video **blogs**; often posted on YouTube channels, with regularly posted video updates.
- **Wikis**: sites that anyone can contribute to, collaborating to create a **crowd-sourced** information set.

Another way that **audiences** create their identity in relation to the **media** is via **fandom**.

Fans of **media** celebrities have long been able to buy **merchandise**, join fan clubs or visit live shows to prove their **fandom**. Now they can meet other fans online to swap information and organise events themselves. These include **comic-con** (comic convention) and **cosplay** (costumed play) events. Fans can also create their own online material, such as fan posters, **trailers**, fiction and videos, emulating their favourite products or using their favourite characters in new scenarios.

The **media** are themselves a topic of conversation, including conversations within other **media** products – television programmes and websites discussing films, for example.

Because people need a **shared understanding** to grasp the encoded **meanings** in **media products**, as our cultures change over time we interpret and respond to **media products** differently. **Societal** and **cultural** changes, for example in relation to gender or **sexuality**, have an impact on how these groups *are* represented in the **media**, and how we *expect* to see them represented. For example, when *Doctor Who* was first launched, **homosexuality** was still illegal in the UK and therefore almost never represented on TV. By comparison, Charlie, a central character in *Class*, is gay and his matter-of-fact **representation** is fairly typical of current **youth TV**.

Link

For more on **fandom** see pages 107–108 of the student book.

Tip ✓

If you are asked to discuss the **social** and **cultural** contexts in which a **media product** was made, you could consider what the original **audience** would have experienced and been aware of, and how this would have affected their potential **responses** to the product.

Knowledge Check 5.9

Unscramble these examples of **audience online identity** and **user-generated content**:

1 kiwi

2 golb

3 mectmon

4 glov

5 pacdots

6 graveleimints

Check It

1 Name one effects theory about passive audiences.

2 Define the term 'cultivation theory'.

3 Name one theory about active audiences.

4 List three potential audience pleasures from a media product.

5 What is two-step flow?

6 What is a moral panic?

7 Do media producers encode or decode their media products?

8 Define the term polysemic.

9 What does Stuart Hall's reception theory say?

10 Briefly explain Blumler and Katz's uses and gratifications theory.

11 What does the term 'oppositional reading' mean?

12 Define the term 'audience positioning'.

13 List the three main methods of audience segmentation.

14 Which of the above methods of audience segmentation focuses on lifestyles and values?

15 Who devised the ABC1 C2DE socio-economic scale?

16 Define the term 'niche audience'.

17 What is the opposite of a niche audience?

18 Give two reasons why media producers want to know the size of their audience.

19 What is a target audience?

20 Why do media companies find it easier to market products that are within known genres?

21 List four different marketing methods.

22 Explain the difference between a taster and a teaser.

23 List at least three media audience research bodies.

24 Which organisation researches and provides data about television audiences?

25 Which organisation researches and provides data about newspaper audiences?

26 Give two examples of primary research methods.

27 What is the difference between quantitative and qualitative research?

28 What does user-generated content (UGC) refer to?

29 List three examples of UGC.

30 Explain the term 'crowd sourcing'.

6 Analysis

Spec Spotlight

Our GCSE exams in Media Studies include questions that allow students to demonstrate their ability to:

- recall information
- draw together information from different areas of the specification
- apply their knowledge and understanding in practical and theoretical contexts
- analyse and compare how media products construct and communicate meaning and generate intended interpretations and responses
- respond through discursive writing to show knowledge and understanding of media issues
- use specialist subject specific terminology appropriately.

AO2: Analyse media products using the theoretical framework of media, including in relation to their contexts, to make judgements and draw conclusions.

The two exam papers together are worth 70% of the available marks for your Media Studies GCSE. Of the available marks for GCSE, 40% (so over half of the marks across the two papers) are for AO2, which focuses on analysis.

Analysis focuses primarily on **Media Languages** and **Media Representations**. The **media forms** studied for these two areas of the **theoretical framework** are:

- **magazines**
- **advertising** and **marketing**
- **newspapers**
- **online, social and participatory media**
- **video games**
- **television**.

The last of these will be assessed in Media Two Section A, including at least one analysis based on a three-minute extract from one of your two television CSPs. The Media One examination paper will contain at least one unseen **media product** that can be reproduced in print form, which you will be required to analyse.

In any analysis, you will be using **semiotics** to discuss how **meanings** have been **constructed** using codes. You will need to be aware of **denotations** (literal **meanings** of **signs** – what it is you can see and hear), and **connotations** (potential **meanings** – what the **signs** suggest to the **audience**).

Analysing unseen products

Nature of related exam questions

Your Media One exam paper will include at least one unseen **media product**, such as an **advertisement**, a **magazine** cover, a **newspaper** page, a DVD cover or a screengrab from a website or video game. There *could* be two unseen products.

For each one, you will be asked a short-answer, possibly multiple choice, question about the product, testing your knowledge and understanding of a key **media** term. Sometimes you will be asked to apply the term to the product to identify an example. Sometimes you will be pointed to the example and asked to correctly identify the term. Questions like this will carry only 1 or 2 marks.

You will then be asked a longer question, such as:

> Analyse the [**media** product] to show how **connotations** communicate **meaning**.

A question such as this is likely to carry 12 marks.

A different form of longer question is to ask you about a specific aspect of **representation**, such as **stereotyping** or one of the **social variables**. For example, you could be asked:

> Explain how **age** is represented in [the **media product**].

Instead of **age**, the question could focus on aspects such as **masculinity**, gender, disability, **ethnicity** and so on. A more narrowly focused question such as this is likely to carry 6 marks.

For each unseen product, you would be asked a short-answer question, testing your understanding of a **key term**, and a longer question testing your analytical skills and ability to apply the theoretical framework. You may be asked to compare the unseen product in some way with one of the CSPs.

Applying media knowledge and understanding to unseen products

Before carrying out an unseen product analysis, make sure you read the question carefully so you know exactly what you are being asked to do. Do you need to focus on the **construction** of **meaning**, or on the **representation** of a specific social group or individual, for example?

Tip

As with all questions carrying more than 2 marks, the assessment criteria are likely to reward analysis responses for the appropriate use of subject specific terminology. If you revise the **media language** terms in Chapter 2 thoroughly, you can apply these to the unseen products.

Tip

Ensure you read all questions carefully and answer exactly what has been asked. If you are asked to analyse a *specific* aspect of **representation**, there will be no marks awarded for analysing other aspects.

When you know what you are looking for, consider which elements in or aspects of the product will be most relevant to the question. Take each of these in turn, using subject specific terminology to describe them and their **denotations**. For each of the elements or aspects, then explain the relevant potential **connotations**.

Example unseen product: advertising and marketing

Potential questions about this **advertising** and **marketing** product include:

1 Identify two **conventions** of a film **marketing** poster.
2 Analyse this **marketing** product to show how different elements communicate **meaning**.
3 Explain how emotion is represented on this poster.

Please note, you would not get all three of these questions about the same product on the same exam paper.

Working through the above questions:

1 Identify two **conventions** of a film **marketing** poster.

Conventions of a film **marketing** poster include:

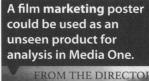

A film **marketing** poster could be used as an unseen product for analysis in Media One.

- the title of the film
- the **tagline**
- a main **image** (almost always including a person)
- the date of the film's forthcoming **release**
- star **billing** (reference to famous actors, directors or **producers**)
- **production** company names
- **website URL**.

You only need to include any two of these to get full marks for the question.

2 Analyse this **marketing** product to show how different **elements** communicate **meaning**.

Check first what the question is asking you to analyse and write about. You are being asked about how different **elements** of the poster convey a **meaning** to the people who see the poster. But what **meanings** are there in the poster? Think about the **meanings** that the poster's designers are trying to convey. They want people to understand firstly that this is a *film* poster, and that the film is being **released** in the summer of 2019. To get this across, they have used the main **conventions** of a film poster so that it is recognisable to the **audience** straightaway. They then want to convey some ideas *about* the film, its **genre** and its **content**, to persuade the **audience** to see the film. To get these **meanings** across they have used a specific **image**, **colour palette**, choice of **copy** (or words) and **fonts**, and **positioning** of each of the elements used.

For this question, the highest level of the marking criteria (carrying 10–12 marks) could be worded as follows:

- Excellent analysis of the product that is detailed and critically engages with the nuanced aspects of how **media language** is used.
- Focus on the intended **meanings** created by the different **elements** of **media language** is thorough and effective throughout.
- Consistent appropriate and effective use of subject specific terminology throughout.

In other words, a high-level response should:

- Discuss *detailed* aspects of the poster. For example, it would not just look at the **image** as a whole, but it would look at details such as the stance of the person (**non-verbal codes**), the fact that they are in silhouette (**technical codes**) and that they are probably looking out to sea (**non-verbal codes** again).
- For *every* detail mentioned, put forward the potential **meanings** for the **audience**. For example, as the person is in silhouette, this means that the **audience** does not know who the specific person is, but they could instead see the person as an 'everyman' figure and identify with the person themselves. The person looking out to sea could connote that they have turned their back on the world behind them and are seeking inspiration elsewhere. You could suggest the different ways in which the title and **tagline anchor** certain interpretations of the **image**.
- Use appropriately, throughout the response, the types of **key terms** emboldened in this book.

3 Explain how emotion is represented on this poster.

Again, check first what the question is asking about. This time your analysis should be focused on the **representation** of emotion within the poster.

For this question, the highest level of the marking criteria (carrying 5–6 marks) could be worded as follows:

- Excellent knowledge and understanding of the **theoretical framework**, demonstrated by consistently effective explanation of emotion.
- Consistently appropriate and effective reference to the *On the Shore* film poster.
- Consistently appropriate and effective use of subject specific terminology throughout.

 Links

For further examples of unseen product analysis, see pages 192 and 194 in Chapter 8 of this book.

 Tip

Make sure you don't spend too long on the questions you find easier, and so run out of time for the questions you find more challenging. In Media One, you have 90 minutes to gain a maximum of 84 marks. In Media Two you have slightly less time, as part of the 90 minutes is spent watching the extract.

In other words, a high-level response should:

- Focus on discussing the **representation** issue (emotion) mentioned in the question. This could be characterised perhaps as despair or loneliness. The answer should focus on how the **representation** of this emotion has been created.

- Refer to details within the unseen **media product** to illustrate what you are discussing. For example, the limited **colour palette** on the film poster **connotes** a sad and sombre mood.

- Use appropriately, throughout the response, the types of **key terms** emboldened in this book.

Knowledge Check 6.1

Taking as many minutes as there are marks available, you could try using the notes above and more details from the product itself to answer each of the three questions on page 124 about the film **marketing** poster.

Knowledge Check 6.2

Example unseen product: **newspaper**

Using the notes on approaching the film marketing poster questions on page 126, answer the following questions about the *Sun*.

1   The cartoon image on this front page of the *Sun* shows the character Homer Simpson looking surprised. Which one of these codes is this an example of?

A. **Action code** ☐

B. **Non-verbal code** ☐

C. **Technical code** ☐

D. **Verbal code** ☐

2   Analyse the front page of the *Sun* to show how connotations communicate meaning.

Practise your analysis skills on this **newspaper front page.**

Analysing Close Study Products

Nature of related exam questions

Exam questions specifically focused on analysis will definitely feature in Media One Section A and Media Two Section A. Other longer-response questions could include aspects of analysis, but they will probably use this to exemplify **media issues** and debates.

Media One Section A

In the sample Media One papers, there are three main styles of analytical questions about the CSPs:

- The first style, worth 8 marks, asks you to analyse specific aspects such as **narrative structures** or **narrative** features in a named CSP.
- The second style, worth 12 marks, asks you to place a specific CSP into the **social** and **cultural** (or other) **contexts** in which it was made, showing how far these are reflected in the product.
- The third style of question, worth 6 marks, gives a statement about **representation** and appeal to a **target audience**, then asks how this is done in a specific CSP.

In addition, a CSP could be used instead of one of the unseen products, including a printed version of this CSP in the paper, with similar questions to the unseen products.

As you can see, all these questions name specific CSPs – usually just one but sometimes a related pair of CSPs. They focus the analysis on a specific aspect. Section A is about **Media Language** and **Representations** but will not cover television, so there are ten CSPs that could be used within this section, covering:

- **magazines**
- **advertising** and **marketing**
- **newspapers**
- **online, social and participatory media**
- **video games**.

Not *all* these CSPs will be covered each year, but you will need to know them all, as any of them *could* be covered.

Media Two Section A – Television

Media Two will start with repeated screenings of a three-minute extract from one of your television CSPs. You will be able to read the questions before these screenings.

The first question will be a short-answer question worth 2 marks, related to the excerpt and assessing the understanding of a **key term** exemplified in that excerpt.

There are likely to be two longer-response tasks requiring analysis of the extract. One is likely to contain a statement about the excerpt, possibly related to the **key term** used in the previous question, and then a question such as 'How is [this issue] represented/demonstrated in the extract?' A task like this would be worth 8 marks.

The second longer-response task could include a statement about the wider context of the CSP or about a specific aspect of the CSP, and then a question such as 'How far does an analysis of the extract show this to be true?' A task like this would be worth 12 marks. A question that starts with 'how far' or 'to what extent' is inviting you to make judgements and draw conclusions.

In the examples above, you would not gain marks for answering the question in relation to other sections of the television CSP. You must answer only in response to the extract where this is stated in the question.

Applying media knowledge and understanding to familiar products

You should be very familiar with your CSPs before entering the exam room, having studied each one in relation to specific areas of the **theoretical framework** and **media contexts** during your course, then having revised them for the exam.

You should understand how each one could act as a case study for the **media form** it exemplifies, and be able to compare and contrast each CSP with the other CSP(s) within the same **media form**.

However, you are not being assessed on your ability to remember and write out an analysis that you have learned, but instead on your ability to carry out your own analysis in the exam. You may already have analysed each CSP with your teacher or your class-mates, but you will probably not have carried out the specific analyses you are being asked for in the exam questions. Each question will point you towards a specific focus for your analysis, so that even where you have learned some of the potential aspects of **Media Language** and **Media Representations** in relation to the CSP, you will need to select the aspects that you consider to be relevant to the set question.

As with the unseen products, start by checking you understand what the question is asking you to do. Then check what you know and understand about the focus of the question. Finally, apply what you know and understand to the product itself, looking for aspects of the product that are the most relevant to the task set.

For example, if the question asks you to analyse the use of **narrative structures** in the CSP, you need to first think what you know about **narrative structures**. Then consider these in relation to the named CSP. Which of the aspects of **narrative structure** can you apply to that CSP – **Propp**'s character roles? The **disruption** of an **equilibrium** and **attempt to repair** the **disruption**? **Enigma**? **Resolution**? Closure? Where in the product do you see any of these in use? How have the **producers** of the CSP used **Media Language** to create this aspect of **narrative structure**?

Tip

Ensure you revise all the CSPs, as you don't know which ones will be covered in the exam questions each year. Television will always be covered in Media Two.

Link

See pages 50–52 of this book, if you're not sure about the use of **narrative structures**.

When you have considered all these questions, you are in a position to answer the question that has been set. Remember that there is no specific number of points you have to make. You are being assessed on the quality of your answer in response to the question that has been set, and your close focus on the CSP.

Knowledge Check 6.3

Try these sample analysis questions.

THE TIMES

SATURDAY
Daily newspaper of the year   5 May 2018 | thetimes.co.uk | No 72527   £1 to subscribers   £1.90

40 best country house hotels
With stunning walks and bike trails
Weekend

Kay Burley
Don't mess with me
Plus **Eat!** recipe pullout
Magazine

MPs call for inquest as Corbyn fails election test

Labour must 'look at itself' after council setback

Francis Elliott Political Editor
Sam Coates, Lucy Fisher

Jeremy Corbyn was criticised by MPs and defeated candidates yesterday for not dealing with antisemitism as his party failed to secure predicted victories in the local elections.

Labour did not win any London councils from the Tories and suffered reverses in former strongholds that voted to leave the EU, in a disappointing performance castigated by one frontbencher as "amateur hour".

The Conservatives were the main beneficiaries from the almost total collapse of Ukip, enabling Theresa May to confound predictions of heavy losses. With all but one set of results declared, Labour was showing a net gain of 57 and the Tories a net loss of 28; the Liberal Democrats were up 75.

Boris Johnson seized on the outcome as evidence that Tory supporters expected and wanted Brexit, saying that Mr Corbyn had been punished for his commitment to remain in a customs union with the EU.

Several Labour figures, however, blamed Mr Corbyn's inaction over antisemitism for his failure to win key councils such as Westminster, Wandsworth and Barnet, Labour's top target.

Barry Rawlings, Barnet's Labour leader, said that too many members of the Jewish community felt that Labour had "failed to deal with antisemitism on

a national level". Adam Langleben, a defeated Labour candidate, called on Mr Corbyn to visit the borough and apologise to its Jewish community.

Jess Phillips, the Labour MP for Birmingham Yardley, said: "The antisemitism problem has been a problem [for Labour] in big metropolitan areas like London and Birmingham. The Labour Party has to look at the results, have a really honest strategy about it to improve it, a real hard honest look at itself."

One Labour frontbencher blamed the "inexperience and hubris" of Mr Corbyn's team for building up unrealistic expectations, including that the party might sweep London. Overall gains would now be presented as a setback, the source said, describing the approach as a "schoolboy error".

Another member of Mr Corbyn's frontbench team told The Times: "At this stage of the parliament, in the aftermath of the home secretary's resignation and all the rest, the opposition should be doing much, much better."

He added: "Our campaign was woeful but we've maxed out London. The problem is that we are not winning provincial England. There was no strategy. Allowing the expectations to get out of kilter was amateur hour."

The Tories themselves lost control of significant councils such as Richmond, southwest London, South Cambridge
Continued on page 2, col 3

Royal appointment **Sir Paul and Lady McCartney at Buckingham Palace yesterday. He received the insignia of the Companion of Honour, an order limited to 65 members**

I've put on a stone in weight!
Caitlin Moran
Magazine

Time to fire up the grill
Bank holiday barbecue
Weekend

Britain's most wanted dad
Fame, fans, four daughters
Magazine

1 Identify two **conventions** of a **newspaper front page** used by The Times.

2 The teaser for Kay Burley's **article** has the **headline** *'Don't mess with me'*. Which one of the following codes is this an example of?

- Action code ☐
- Non-verbal code ☐
- Post-production code ☐
- Verbal code ☐

3 Explain how **femininity** is represented on the **front page** of *The Times*.

4 **Newspapers** often create representations of **important people** (celebrities, politicians and others) specifically to appeal to their **target audiences**. How has this been done on the **front page** of *The Times* (CSP)?

Tip

For most analysis questions, there will be more to discuss than you have time or space for. Choose the aspects that seem the most relevant or interesting, and discuss these in detail, rather than trying to cover everything you can.

5 Analyse the **front page** of *The Times* to show how different elements communicate **meaning**.

7 Revising the CSPs

Spec Spotlight

The CSPs will address the requirement that students engage with products that:

- possess cultural, social and historical significance in terms of critical acclaim and/or audience popularity
- reflect and illuminate the theoretical framework for the study of media
- demonstrate contrasts in terms of perceived quality, form and structure
- provide rich and challenging opportunities for interpretation and analysis, enabling students to develop a detailed understanding of how the media communicate meanings
- are from different historical periods
- are intended for different audiences
- demonstrate emerging, future developments of the media
- are not necessarily the type of products which students would normally engage.

The focus of study is not the products themselves but, rather, the theoretical framework and contexts of media. Exam questions will focus on the theoretical framework and contexts of the media but students will be expected to answer with reference to or analysis of relevant CSPs.

These products should be seen as a vehicle for the delivery of the specification, rather than products to be 'learned' in detail.

Targeted products: Media Language and Media Representations

Magazines

Link

See also Chapter 2 page 35 of this book for the **technical codes** for a **magazine front cover**.

Rapid Recap

You need to be able to compare and contrast the two **magazines** shown on the next page to discover:

- The relationship between each **magazine** and their **social** and **cultural contexts** of production – including the different **audiences** for each product.
- The **issues** that each **magazine** prefers to deal with.
- The **values** and **beliefs** implied by the contents and **presentation**.

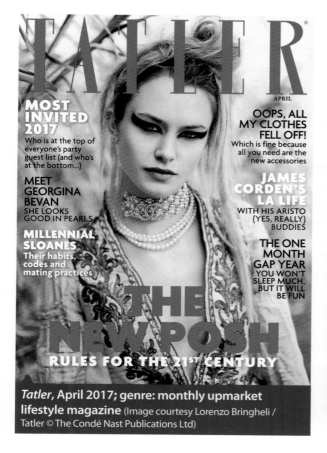

Tatler, April 2017; **genre: monthly upmarket lifestyle magazine** (Image courtesy Lorenzo Bringheli / Tatler © The Condé Nast Publications Ltd)

Reveal, 18 March 2017; **genre: weekly lifestyle/celebrity gossip magazine**

Media Language

You need to be able to recognise, analyse and discuss:

- The **conventions** of a **magazine** cover and the extent to which each cover conforms to these or rejects them.
- The **genre** features that identify the particular category of **magazine**.
- The **design** and **layout** of the cover, including:
  - **typography**
  - use of colour
  - use of **language**
  - choice of content elements
  - **juxtaposition** of these elements.
- How the **media language targets** and addresses the **audience**.
- How **narrative devices** tempt buyers to **acquire** and read the **magazine**.

> **Link**
>
> For more on *Tatler* and *Reveal* **front covers** see pages 207–209 of the student book.

> **Link**
>
> For more on the **Media Representations** of *Tatler* and *Reveal* see pages 209–210 of the student book.

Link

For more on **media packs** see page 91 of the student book.

Media Representations

You need to be able to analyse and discuss:

- How the chosen people, **issues** and ideas have been **represented**.
- How and why different **social groups** have been **stereotyped**, **under-represented** or **misrepresented**.
- How and why different **audiences** will **interpret** these **representations** differently.

Contextual and other key information

As you are studying these two products for **Media Language** and **Media Representations**, most of the key information is held within the CSPs themselves. It is helpful to know a little about the **audience**, however, so that you can analyse how the **media language** and **representations** used within the products help to target their **audiences**.

Tatler was first published in 1901 and has been a monthly **magazine** since 1977.

In addition to the information on the left, the October 2018 *Tatler* **media pack** states that:

- 96% of *Tatler's* readers own designer fashion.
- 81% of *Tatler's* readers own designer shoes and accessories.
- 75% own high-end watches or jewellery.
- 96% own premium beauty products.
- 97% consider themselves luxury travellers, with an average of eight trips in the UK and seven trips abroad each year.

Tatler is aimed at upper-class and upper-middle-class women, who are interested in designer fashion and travel.

Reveal was launched in 2004 and closed in 2018 due to a decline in sales, with the last issue going on sale in October 2018.

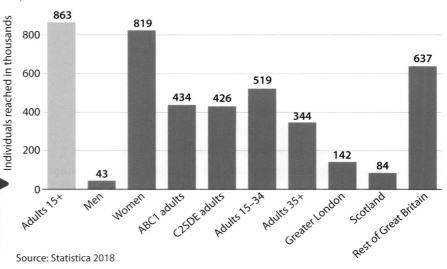

Source: Statistica 2018

The graph for the **audience reach** of *Reveal* **magazine** (in print and online) in 2015–2016 shows that within that **audience**:

- 95% were female
- 50% were ABC1 and 50% were C2DE
- 60% were aged 15–34
- 16% were based in Greater London.

Reveal was aimed at working-class and middle-class women, who were interested in high street fashion and celebrity gossip.

Tip

Your knowledge and understanding of **magazines** and the two related CSPs can be assessed in Media One Section A: Language and Representations.

Knowledge Check 7.1

Thinking about the person viewing the **magazine**, the people represented on the cover (both in the text and the **images**), and the publication itself, as characters, what **narratives** are being put forward on each **front cover**? Consider the following:

1 **Narrative structure**
   a. Is there an initial **equilibrium**?
   b. Are there obstacles, or **disruption**s to the **equilibrium**?
   c. If so, how can the reader find a **resolution** to the **disruption**?

2 **Propp**'s theories
   a. Who is the main **protagonist**?
   b. What **quest** is the **front cover** sending them on?
   c. Who or what is the **helper** or **donor**?
   d. If they complete the **quest** successfully, what prize(s) do they gain?

3 Other **narrative** theories
   a. What **binary opposites** are suggested or implied?
   b. What **enigmas** are set up?

Complete the table to provide a direct comparison between the two **magazine** covers on page 133 – the first row has been completed for you.

Aspect or element to be analysed	*Tatler* front cover		*Reveal* front cover	
Target audience:		Target audience:		
	Sign **What can you see?**	**Connotation** **What does it mean?**	**Sign** **What can you see?**	**Connotation** **What does it mean?**
Number of **images** used	One **image**	Uncluttered, straightforward publication	Eight **images**	The publication is bursting with stories
Content of **images**	Model, MCU, looking directly at the camera, in natural surroundings			
Colours used				
Font style in **masthead**	**Serif font**, all capitals, pink			
Font styles in **cover lines**				
Main **cover line**	The new posh Rules for the 21st century		Katie plots secret meetings with Pete	
Content of **cover lines**				
Use of punctuation	Brackets used in 2 **cover lines** Commas used in 4 **cover lines**		Quote marks used in 4 **cover lines** Exclamation marks used in 4 **cover lines**	
Vocabulary			Familiar and friendly, slang and abbreviations, first names	
Juxtaposition of elements on the page	Type is ranged around the outside of the cover, not obscuring the model			
Other features such as price and graphics				

Advertising and marketing

Rapid Recap

Three products:

- OMO print advert from *Woman's Own* **magazine**, 5 May 1955
- Galaxy 'Audrey Hepburn' television advertisement
- NHS Blood and Transplant online campaign video 'Represent featuring Lady Leshurr'.

OMO, print washing powder advert, 1955

QR code for the 'Represent' online video

NHS Blood and Transplant online 'Represent' campaign, 2016

Galaxy, TV confectionery advert, 2013

QR code for the Galaxy 'Audrey Hepburn' television advert

Links

See also:

- Chapter 1 page 19 for some of the **denotations** and **connotations** of the OMO advert.
- Chapter 1 page 20 for some questions about **denotations** and **connotations** in the 'Represent' online video.
- Chapter 2 pages 28–32 for the **technical codes** for **moving image** products.
- Chapter 2 pages 33–34 and 38 for the **technical codes** for a print advertisement.
- Chapter 3 pages 61 and 64 for questions about the **representation** of the product in the Galaxy advert.
- Chapter 3 page 82 for suggestions about possible different **audiences** for the Galaxy advert.

Overall study and contexts of the media

You need to be able to analyse, compare and contrast the three adverts to discover:

- How their **historical**, **social**, **cultural** and **political contexts** have affected their **construction**. In other words, how the **media language** and **media representations** reflect the **social**, **cultural** and **historical contexts** in which the **advertisements** were made.

- The powerful influence of changing **social values** and **beliefs** on **advertisements**, particularly:

  - How **political** changes have played a role in the developments that make the OMO advert seem outdated and unusual, especially in terms of **gender representation**.

- How **CGI** and **intertextual references** to a dead celebrity have been used in the Galaxy 'Audrey Hepburn' advert, and the **issues** this raises of the link between **advertising**, identity and consumerism.
- How the **targeting** of a **niche** (BAME) **audience** has influenced the **construction** of the 'Represent' advert, and the **issues** this raises about the social function of some promotional campaigns and the impact they can have on society.

Media Language

You need to be able to recognise, analyse and discuss:

- The codes and **conventions** of **advertisements** on different **media platforms** and how these communicate meaning.
- The **connotations** and **denotations** of the various **signs** that make up the **advertisements**.
- How the following contribute to the **meaning** of the **advertisements**:
  - **layout** and **design**
  - **typography**
  - non-verbal communication (body language)
  - use of **language**.
- The techniques of persuasion – how a persuasive **message** is **constructed** using **media language**, and what that **message** is.
- The **narrative structure** of the advert.
- How **narrative** theories can be applied – such as **Propp**.
- How the **narrative** creates a point of view in each case.
- OMO: how **media language positions** the **target audience**, and the impacts this has on different **audiences** over time.
- Galaxy and 'Represent': how **intertextuality** has been used.
- 'Represent': what the **genre** (including potential **hybrid genres**) of the product is, and how **media language** is used to convey this.

Media Representations

You need to be able to analyse and discuss:

- The **representation** of **gender**, particularly **femininity** but also the implied **representation** of **masculinity**.
- The **representation** of **ethnicity**, **age**, **social class**, disability and **place** in the 'Represent' advert.
- How the Galaxy advert represents a **place**, **celebrity persona**, **social class**, **age**, historical period and a sense of nostalgia.
- The use and function of **stereotypes**, and their effectiveness.
- The **representation** of the products (OMO or Galaxy chocolate).
- How the adverts **construct** a version of reality.

Link

See Chapter 2 page 53 of this book for **Propp**'s theory.

You could focus on the three main characters from each advert to analyse the representations of femininity.

Link

See Chapter 3 page 66 of this book for a confectionery advert from the 1950s to compare with the 1950s OMO advert and the 2013 Galaxy advert.

- The viewpoints, messages, **values** and beliefs **communicated** by the processes of **selection**, **construction** and **mediation** – in other words, what viewpoints have been put across by the choices made in **constructing** the adverts.
- What is unfamiliar and what is familiar about the 1950s world of the OMO advert.
- How different **audiences' interpretations** of the adverts (including your own) are influenced by their experiences and beliefs.
- How the advertisements **position audience** members in relation to **personal identity**, particularly their own.

Contextual and other key information

As you are studying these two products for **Media Language** and **Media Representations**, most of the key information is held within the CSPs themselves. It is helpful to know a little about the **audience**, however, so that you can analyse how the **media language** and **representations** within the products help to **target** and **position** their **audiences**.

The OMO advert appeared in *Woman's Own*, one of the UK's most famous women's weekly **magazines**. The **magazine targeted** lower-middle-class and working-class women, and still prides itself on being a **magazine** that '*mirrors the lives of its readers and keeps at its heart their key interests in getting value for money and sound advice*' (*Woman's Own* (2018) https://www.ti-media.com//wp-content/uploads/2015/08/Womans-Own.pdf). For example, the **magazine** in the 1950s offered readers dress patterns and knitting instructions so that they could make designer clothes they would otherwise not be able to afford.

Prior to marriage, most of the **target audience** would have had jobs in offices or shops. The majority of the **magazine's** married readers in 1955 would not have had paid employment, as this would have been seen as insulting to their husbands who were supposed to provide for their family. They were therefore mostly full-time housewives, looking after the home and family. The UK was still a highly patriarchal society in 1955; one in which men held positions of power and authority, and in which women were exploited. The **mass media**, including **advertising**, played an important role in **reinforcing** the **values** and **beliefs** linked to male **domination**.

Actors Jenny Ishammar and Lou-Hélène Barbry during the filming of the Galaxy advert.

The Galaxy advert was shown on TV in Ireland and the UK from 2013 onwards. It targeted a middle-class female **audience**. Audrey Hepburn, a glamorous Hollywood actress in the 1950s and 1960s, had died in 1993 (20 years before the ad was made and broadcast) at the age of 62. She was re-created in the advert using two similar-looking actors and lots of **CGI**. One of her most famous films was *Roman Holiday*, set in Italy. The advert is set on the Amalfi coast, also in Italy. This **setting connotes** luxury, glamour and status to a British and Irish **audience**, and some commentators online have said the advert would work just as effectively as a perfume advert. The advert is more popular with older women who are more familiar with Audrey Hepburn as a famous film star.

The 'Represent' video was created as a **collaboration** between NHS Blood and Transplant and MOBO (Music of Black Origin), to attract young black and Asian people in the UK to give blood and sign the organ donor register. The song was written and performed by UK grime artist Lady Leshurr, a 2016 MOBO Award nominee. The people featured in the video include: Olympian boxer Nicola Adams MBE, TV **presenter** and wheelchair basketball player Ade Adepitan, MOBO's CEO Kanya King MBE, model Mariah Idrissi, Chuka Umunna MP, cycling and triathlon sports coach Dawn Hunter, the London Community Gospel Choir, and Queen's Park Rangers' footballer Gianni Crichlow. The video's producers deliberately chose these people (and more) as 'key role models and influencers from within the BAME community' (Mullenlowe (2018) https://www.mullenlowelondon.com/our-work/represent/).

Tip

Your knowledge and understanding of **advertising** and **marketing** and the three related CSPs can be assessed in Media One Section A: Language and Representations.

Knowledge Check 7.3

Can you apply the **advertisers'** acronym **AIDA** to each **advertising** and **marketing** CSP? What persuasive techniques have they used for each part of this process?

	OMO print advert	Galaxy 'Audrey Hepburn' TV advert	NHS Blood and Trasplant advert
Attention: make people notice the advert			
Interest: make people want to know more about the product or service			
Desire: make people want to buy the product or engage with the service			
Action: tell people how to act on the advert, to buy the product or engage with the service			

Answer the following questions about **representation**.

1 How are women **represented** in each advert?

2 How are men **represented** in each advert, either actually or
   by implication?

3 How has the 'Represent' video **constructed positive representations**
   of various **social groups** to convey its overall message?

4 How are celebrities used and represented in the Galaxy advert and
   'Represent' video?

5 What is the intended meaning of the implied celebrity **endorsement**?

Targeted products: Media Industries and Media Audiences

Radio

Rapid Recap

Two products:

- Radio 1 launch day – Tony Blackburn's breakfast show, September 1967 (excerpts)
- Beats 1 Radio – *Julie Adenuga* show.

Radio 1 launch day with Tony Blackburn: the UK-based broadcast pop music radio station, launched September 1967 by the BBC.

The *Julie Adenuga* show on Beats 1 Radio; a global online music radio station, launched June 2015 by Apple.

QR code for Radio Rewind webpage with clips from the Radio 1 launch day.

QR code for Beats 1 Radio YouTube channel.

Links

See also:

Chapter 2 pages 31–32 for the **technical codes** of an audio product. Although you are not being assessed on **Media Language** for these CSPs, these may be useful when discussing specific details in relation to **audience targeting** and appeal.

Chapter 5 page 112 for a description of the **target audience** for Radio 1's launch day.

Chapter 5 pages 90–91 for information about the BBC, its licence and **public service remit**.

Overall study and contexts of the media

You need to be able to compare and contrast the two **radio** CSPs to discover:

- The role and relevance of **radio** in the online **media landscape**, comparing Radio 1 at the time of its launch with Beats 1 Radio and other **streaming services**.
- The historical developments in **music radio**, specifically **radio** designed to cater for the **music** tastes of a youth audience:
  - The **political context** for the launch of Radio 1 – the role of **pirate radio** in the 1960s, and its suppression by the government before Radio 1's launch.
  - Why the launch of Radio 1 in 1967 was an important turning point in the history of **radio**.
  - How Radio 1 has coped with changing demands and pressures since 1967.
- Modern trends and developments in **music radio**, specifically **radio** designed to cater for the **music** tastes of a youth audience.

Link

For more about Tony Blackburn's and Julie Adenuga's shows see pages 198–200 of the student book.

Media Industries

You need to understand and be able to discuss:

- How the BBC was **funded** in 1967, and how Radio 1 was influenced by the BBC's role as a public service provider.
- Why the BBC made significant changes to its **radio** provision at that time.
- Why Apple got involved in **music radio**:
  - Why Apple wanted to **diversify** into providing **music** content as well as hardware.
  - How Apple's decisions were influenced by **cultural** and **technological developments**.
- The **issues** linked to **ownership**, **globalisation** and **convergence**.
- Who the **presenters** were/are for each **radio** station, and how they influenced the style and **music** of the station.
- The success of each station at launch and over the subsequent years.

- The rules and **regulations** constraining each station:
  - The restrictions on **needletime** for the BBC in 1967.
  - The need for BBC stations to inform, educate and entertain.
  - The freedom (or not) given to each Beats 1 **presenter** to select their own **music** choices.
- How much of a threat Beats 1 and **streaming music** services are to **traditional media industries**.

Media Audiences

You need to understand and be able to discuss:

- The **target audience** for each CSP show.
- *How* each CSP **radio** station targets its **audience** and what appeals the particular CSP shows offer(ed).
- How the **radio** stations fulfil the needs of their listeners and contribute to their sense of identity.
- How each CSP show **positioned** the **audience**.
- The **preferred reading** of each show.
- How the needs and tastes of the youth audience were perceived by the BBC in 1967.
- The differences between how young people could access **music** in 1967 and how they can access **music** today.
- The differences between how young people used music in 1967 and how they use **music** today.
- How the **audience** can actively engage with each CSP station.
- Whether the **uses and gratifications theory** is useful when looking at the **audiences** of these two stations.

Contextual and other key information

You will not be assessed on your ability to memorise the following information, but you could use your understanding of some of these points in support of a discussion question about **radio** industries and/or **audiences**.

Radio 1 is a **national** BBC **radio** station, originally broadcast on 247m MW (medium wave), and now broadcasting on FM **radio** 97.7–99.7 MHz, DAB (digital audio broadcasting) **radio**, RDS, Freeview, Freesat, Sky, Virgin Media and as a webstream at http://www.bbc.co.uk/radio/player/bbc_radio_one.

QR code for Radio 1 webstream player

The BBC had a monopoly on legal **radio** services in the UK from 1927 to 1973, with a small number of **national** services.

Radio 1 was launched after **pirate radio stations** such as Radio Caroline and Radio London proved popular with youth audiences from 1964 onwards. These initially broadcast from sea forts – abandoned off-shore military platforms – and from ships moored off the coast of Britain. This avoided the need for a UK broadcasting licence, which they would not have been able to obtain but without which they would have been broadcasting illegally, so could have been shut down. The Marine Offences Act of 1967 made it unlawful for a British citizen to work for such a station after 14 August 1967. The **pirate radio stations** had estimated collective audiences of 10 to 15 million, who were not being **targeted** by BBC **radio** at all.

BBC **radio** was reorganised from 30 September 1967 as shown below.

BBC Home Service
Mainly speech-based **radio**, including regional programming, news, drama and topical discussion, and school programmes

BBC Radio 4
Curious and intelligent adult **audience**; news, current affairs, arts, drama and comedy

BBC Radio 1
Targets 15–29 year olds; pop and rock **music**, including the Top 40 singles

BBC Light Programme
Light entertainment and **music**

BBC Radio 2
Adult **audience**; 'middle of the road' **music** – easy listening, folk, jazz and light entertainment

BBC Third Programme
Culture and the arts, including non-topical talk programmes and serious drama

BBC Radio 3
Educated adult **audience**; arts and high culture – classical, opera, jazz and world **music**

BBC Music Programme
Classical **music** and live sports coverage

The four new BBC **radio** stations initially had a shared **needletime** of seven hours a day – in other words, they could only play seven hours of *recorded* **music** between them. This was agreed between the BBC, PPL (Phonographic Performance Limited: representing the record companies) and the Musicians' Union, to protect the use of *live* **music** and the livelihoods of musicians. As **music** was a key component of many **radio** shows, musicians were employed to play much of this live in addition to the seven hours of needletime, and the agreement secured their jobs.

Pirate radio stations had no **needletime** agreements and played non-stop recorded **music**. Their **presenters** (or disc jockeys – DJs) were also used to being entertainers rather than announcers, working without scripts. The BBC, up to this point, had announcers rather than DJs, and the announcers used prepared scripts throughout each show. Tony Blackburn had been a DJ on both Radio Caroline and Radio London (both **pirate radio stations**), so he brought the same **informal** style of presentation to Radio 1.

Local BBC stations were launched from November 1967 onwards.

Local commercial **radio** stations were first granted licences in 1973.

Three **national** commercial **radio** stations were allowed to broadcast in 1992 – Classic FM, Talk Radio and Virgin Radio.

The first internet **radio** station, Virgin Radio, was launched in 1996.

DAB **radios** were available from 1999 onwards.

Music **streaming services** were available from the early 2000s, with Spotify launching in 2008.

By 2016, 45.5% of **radio** listening in the UK was via **digital platforms** – DAB, internet **radio** and television. The rest was via analogue FM radios (Hannah Bouckley (2018) http://home.bt.com/tech-gadgets/internet/broadband/from-marconi-and-the-transistor-radio-to-dab-the-history-of-radio-in-the-uk-11364015764901).

Over 68 billion songs were streamed in the UK in 2017, an increase of 52% on 2016 (British Phonographic Industry, quoted on Nick Durrant (2018) https://www.moneysavingexpert.com/shopping/free-music/).

There are now around 600 licensed **radio** stations broadcasting in the UK, plus onshore **pirate radio stations** and internet-only streaming stations. Over 400 of these broadcast stations can be accessed via Radioplayer online at http://www.radioplayer.co.uk/.

QR code to access Radioplayer

Beats 1 Radio is **wholly owned** by Apple. The global **radio** station was launched in June 2015, broadcasts to over 100 countries and is available without **subscription** via iTunes or Apple Music on any iOS device. In other words, it is free to listen to. A **subscription** to Apple Music is needed on an Android device, which at time of writing costs £9.99 per month. The **target audience** is described by Apple as *'people who enjoy listening to new music and love music in general'* (Guiding Tech (2018) https://www.guidingtech.com/46483/beats-1-apple-music-radio-differences-explained/).

As it is part of the Apple Music service, it has direct links to other **music** products that listeners can pay for: **music downloads** and **subscription streaming**. It features pop, rap and indie **music**, with a focus on *new* **music**, both from new and established artists. Most shows focus on specific **music** genres or musical **cultures**.

Julie Adenuga's show focuses on **music** from the UK. Adenuga is the sister of grime artists JME and Skepta, and previously presented the drive time show on London-based Rinse FM as well as a UK rap and grime **music** television show on Channel AKA. Rinse FM, which started as a **pirate radio station** but gained a legal licence in 2010, focuses on UK dance **music**, such as grime, dubstep and house.

Beats 1's focus on new **music**, personally recommended by lively **presenters**, gives **consumers** of Apple Music and iTunes a guide as to what to look for when they are using those services. Many commentators online see it as a bigger threat to Spotify than to Capital FM or Radio 1 (Sarah Jane Griffiths (2015) https://www.bbc.co.uk/news/entertainment-arts-33064181).

Both Radio 1 (through Radioplayer or the show's playlist on the BBC website) and Beats 1 Radio (through its playlists) allow listeners to add songs they like to a personal online directory, to buy or stream later.

BBC Radio 1 **reached** 10.7 million listeners aged 10+ in the first part of 2018, with the breakfast show having a weekly **audience** of 6.16 million (BBC (2018) https://www.bbc.co.uk/mediacentre/latestnews/2018/q2-rajar). Apple claimed in 2017 that Beats 1 was the biggest **radio** station in the world, but they have not supplied **listener figures** (9T-5Mac (2017) https://9to5mac.com/2017/03/26/apple-music-beats-1-listening-numbers/).

Radio 1 is available across a number of platforms.

Knowledge Check 7.5

Based on your listening to each show, or reading of a transcript, complete the following comparison.

	BBC Radio 1 launch: Tony Blackburn	Beats 1 Radio: Julie Adenuga
Target audience		
How does the **presenter** address the **audience**?		
What appeals does the show and its **presenter** have for the **audience**?		
How are the **audience** **positioned** by the show? What **identity** does it offer them?		
How are the **audience** included in the show? How can they actively engage with it?		
What is the **preferred reading** of the show?		

Knowledge Check 7.6

Answer the following questions about **radio**.

1 What **uses and gratifications** are available to **audiences** of the **radio** CSPs?

2 How have **technological developments** and **convergence** led to the launch of Beats 1?

3 How has Radio 1 used **technological developments** to try to keep pace with its rivals and with modern **audiences**?

Tip

Your knowledge and understanding of **radio** and the two related CSPs can be assessed in Media One Section B: Industries and Audiences.

Music video

Rapid Recap

Two products:

- Arctic Monkeys – 'I Bet You Look Good on the Dancefloor' (2005)
- One Direction – 'History' (2015).

Although you are not being assessed on **Media Language** for these CSPs, the **technical codes** may be useful when discussing specific details in relation to **audience targeting** and appeal.

Link

See also Chapter 2 pages 28–32 of this book for the **technical codes** of a **moving image** product.

Arctic Monkeys (left) and One Direction (right) music videos

QR code to Arctic Monkeys – 'I Bet You Look Good on the Dancefloor'

QR code to One Direction – 'History'

Overall study and contexts of the media

You need to be able to compare and contrast the two **music video** CSPs to discover:

- The wider **cultural** debate about the merit of 'manufactured' pop **music** such as boy bands and TV reality show winners versus the supposedly 'authentic' indie bands and rap artists.
- The effects of **convergence** between **media industries**, the role of video in r**eaching audiences** and the relationship between producers and **audiences**.
- How Arctic Monkeys may be seen as a case study comparable with other key events in the history of popular **music** such as The Beatles forming their own **record label** and the rejection of stadium and pomp rock by the punk explosion.

Media Industries

You need to understand and be able to discuss:

- Why the Arctic Monkeys' video exemplified a turning point in the relationship between the **music** industry, artists and fans:
  - How the video relates to emerging, future developments in the **media** as it represents a change in the way that artists could, potentially, build and communicate with an **audience**.
  - How **technological developments** enabled bands/artists such as Arctic Monkeys to self-produce their own artistic output.
  - The implications of these challenges to **mainstream music** producers and publishers.
- The relationship between the One Direction video (and the timing of its **release**) and their other singles and albums.
- How influential record companies (including Simon Cowell's Syco) are in determining the form and content of **music videos** such as 'History'.
- The role played by **music video** in One Direction's huge global success.
- How **music videos** are **rated** and **regulated** in the UK.

Media Audiences

You need to understand and be able to discuss:

- How the two bands have used **music video** to project their **image**:
  - The nature of **music video** as a primary means of **projecting** an **image** for bands/artists.
  - How much control they have over their **image** and the different **perceptions** of that **image**.
  - What assumptions the video makers have made about the **target audience**.

- How the two CSP videos **target** and address their **audiences**.
- The pleasures and rewards of **music videos** for their **audiences**.
- How **audiences consume** and use **music videos**.
- How and why **audience responses** to the videos vary, and whether these **responses** change over time.
- How Arctic Monkeys exploited the online presence and **niche** nature of their fanbase.

Contextual and other key information

You will not be assessed on your ability to memorise the following information, but you could use your understanding of some of these points in support of a discussion question about **music video** industries and/or **audiences**.

Music videos: Music videos are a way of presenting the **brand** of the **music** artists, presenting them as a **commodity** to be bought by the **target audience**. The style and content of many **music videos** are controlled by the record companies the artists are signed to.

Music videos were first created to allow artists to be seen on TV shows even when they were touring, or to be seen by their fans without having to make live appearances. They grew in number and complexity after the launch of MTV – Music TV channel – in 1981. Now they are most often viewed via **social media platforms**, especially YouTube. As YouTube is free to use, this means the videos of unsigned, largely unknown bands can be viewed on the same **platform** as bands that have major commercial success.

On YouTube and other **social media platforms** there is no requirement to have age ratings for videos. However, there is a **pilot scheme** between the BBFC, Sony Music UK, Universal Music UK and Warner Music UK to post **age ratings** next to their **music videos**, to allow **audiences** to choose whether or not to watch. **Social media platforms** use a combination of their employees, computer algorithms and direct reporting from the **audience** to decide when videos break their own codes of decency and legality. If **music videos** are made available on DVD in the UK, **BBFC** must provide **age rating** certification.

Prior to Arctic Monkeys' rise to fame, there had been controversy over **peer-to-peer file-sharing sites** such as Napster (the original site of that name was started in 1999 and forced to close in 2001 because of a lawsuit over illegal file-sharing). **Record labels** complained they were losing out on **revenue**. In 2004 iTunes was launched, allowing for the legal, paid-for **downloading** of **music** tracks. Arctic Monkeys shared their first **demo recording** via iTunes, but also posted it on their website for free, as well as distributing 500 free CD copies.

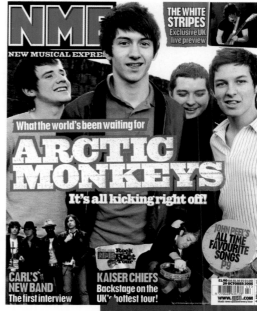

Arctic Monkeys were featured on the front page of *NME* two weeks before their first single was released. (Image © www.ti-mediacontent.com)

 Link

For more on Arctic Monkeys see pages 212–214 of the student book.

This YouTube page for Calvin Harris's *Open Wide* video shows an age rating as the 'partner rating' in the information about the video.

Arctic Monkeys' first video features the band playing live and has **camera operators** clearly in shot.

Arctic Monkeys: Arctic Monkeys' 'I Bet You Look Good on the Dancefloor' was the band's first official single (on the Domino **record label**), **released** on 17 October 2005. It went straight to number one in the charts and sold over 174,000 copies.

The band had built their initial fame and reputation playing live around Sheffield and giving away free copies of their **demo recordings**. They became known as a band worth seeing, and their gigs sold out because details were shared via text and the internet. Fans left their CDs in public places for others to pick up. The fans also shared the recordings online and posted them on a fan-made account on the **social media** site MySpace.

The band's rise to fame attracted the interest of BBC **radio**, the British **tabloid newspapers** and **record labels**. They turned down several recording contract offers before signing to Domino, because they felt the label's owner, Laurence Bell, shared their DIY mentality and wasn't just in it for the money. He only signed bands he personally liked and ran the business from his home.

The video looks **low budget** and shows the band playing the song live in a warehouse-like space. **Camera operators**, cables and speakers are clearly in shot. The band mainly ignores the cameras, instead focusing on their instruments or looking out at an imagined **audience** within the venue. Watching the video is similar to being at one of their gigs, except that there are no other fans in the way. It emphasises their **image** thus far – an authentic, down-to-earth band who enjoy playing live **music**.

They owed their initial success to their fans' online **social networking**, and the ability to distribute and promote their **music** widely at very little cost.

One Direction: One Direction was formed for the **reality TV** talent show *The X Factor* in 2010. The **franchise** for *The X Factor* is owned by Simon Cowell and his company Syco TV. All five soon-to-be-members of One Direction had auditioned for the show as solo candidates but were put together on the show to form a boy band. They came third, but were so popular with the show's fans that they were signed to Simon Cowell's Syco Music **record label** (a **subsidiary** of Syco, which has a **distribution deal** with Sony Music) for a reported £2 million. Syco Music has the exclusive right to sign winners and finalists of *The X Factor* and *Got Talent* (another Syco creation).

One Direction **released** five albums over the next five years, with 'History' being the third and final single from the fifth album.

It has been said, including by Sonny Takhar, the former chief executive officer of Syco Music, that the band owe much of its success worldwide to **social media**. Music fans now use **social media**, including YouTube, in the way they previously used **radio**, but are able to share what they enjoy with others.

The band members had (and still have) group and individual prominent online presences, especially on Twitter. This enabled fans to feel as though they were in personal contact with the band, enjoying a closer relationship than previous generations of music lovers. The group's Twitter account had ten million followers by February 2013. In October 2018 it had 31.3 million followers. All the individual members of the band had between 33 and 40 million followers at the same point.

The 2015 One Direction 'History' video shows the band performing in front of a blank brick wall, **intercut** with black and white footage from the previous five years. It therefore self-referentially covers the band's own history since their creation during *The X Factor*. Their debt to Simon Cowell is clearly acknowledged in the video, as is the adoration of their fans who are included in many of the shots.

In comparison to the Arctic Monkeys' video, One Direction is clearly not performing live, as there are no microphones. They look directly at the camera, singing straight to the viewer, emphasising the personal **direct address** of the chorus lyrics.

The 'History' video includes references to the band's history, their debt to Simon Cowell and their fans, as well as footage of them singing to the camera.

 **Link**

For more on One Direction see pages 214–217 of the student book.

	Arctic Monkeys – 'I Bet you Look Good on the Dancefloor'	One Direction – 'History'
Target audience		
How does the video address the **audience**?		
What appeals does the video have for the **audience**?		
How are the **audience** positioned by the video? What **identity** does it give them?		
How are the **audience** included in the video? How can they actively engage with it?		
What is the **preferred reading** of the video?		

Knowledge Check 7.8

Answer the following questions about Arctic Monkeys and One Direction.

1 What were the implications of Arctic Monkeys' success for **mainstream music** producers and **publishers**?

2 How did **technological developments** and **convergence** enable each band to succeed?

3 What was the role of the **audience** in helping each band to establish success?

Tip

Your knowledge and understanding of **music video** and the two related CSPs can be assessed in Media One Section B: Industries and Audiences.

Film

Film poster for *Doctor Strange*

Two products:

- *Doctor Strange* (dir. Scott Derrickson, 2016)
- *I, Daniel Blake* (dir. Ken Loach, 2016).

Overall study and contexts of the media

You need to be able to compare and contrast the two film industry CSPs to discover:

- The impact of film **funding**, the effects of ownership, rating and **regulation**, the global scale of the film industry as well as other industry **issues**.
- The **political** and **cultural contexts** of film **funding**, especially as nations and regions compete for business.
- The **issues** surrounding the **production**, distribution and **exhibition** of film in the **digital** age.
- **Issues** surrounding the lack of access to **funding** for **independent film production**, and difficulties of distribution and **exhibition** for **limited audience** films.

Media Industries

You need to understand and be able to discuss:

- The **production** companies involved in the making of the two film CSPs.
- The terms '**blockbuster**' and '**independent cinema**'.
- The **production budgets** of the two films.
- How their **audiences** were **targeted**.
- How '**star power**' and '**director power**' can be used to **market** a film.
- How the two films were **released**.
- How successful they were at the **box office**.
- What certification each film received and why.
- What **merchandising tie-ins** were associated with each film.
- Which **multimedia platforms** supported the **marketing** of each film.
- How many countries each film was distributed to.
- Which **multimedia platforms** support the **exhibition** of each film.

Film poster for *I, Daniel Blake*

- How the above helps with understanding the nature of **globalisation**.
- What effect the **domination** of Hollywood has on national cinema production worldwide.

Contextual and other key information

You will not be assessed on your ability to memorise the following information, but you could use your understanding of some of these points in support of a discussion question about the film industry.

Doctor Strange: *Doctor Strange* is the 14th film in the Marvel *Avengers* series, otherwise called the Marvel Cinematic Universe (MCU). It had a **budget** of $165 million and took over $677 million at cinema box offices. It is referred to as a Hollywood **blockbuster**: a highly popular, high-**budget** film with star actors, which makes a huge profit for its owners.

Marvel Studios is a **wholly-owned** USA-based **subsidiary** of the Walt Disney Company. By buying Marvel Entertainment in 2009 for $4 billion, Disney **acquired** the **intellectual property** of Marvel Comics. Marvel Studios' films are distributed to cinemas by Walt Disney Studios Motion Pictures.

Marvel Studios first brought in writers for a *Doctor Strange* film in 2009, and in 2013 finally confirmed the film would go into **production**. The **production schedule** was moved to allow Benedict Cumberbatch to star as Doctor Strange. The role of The Ancient One was specially adapted and written with Tilda Swinton in mind, before she was asked to play the role.

Filming took place from 4 November 2015 in Nepal to 3 April 2016 in New York City. **Location shooting** also took place in Hong Kong, Oxford, Kent and London. **Studio shooting** took place at Longcross and Shepperton Studios in the UK. Twenty-one **sets** were built at Longcross.

The film uses a huge amount of **CGI**, with eight **special effects** companies contributing to 1,450 effects shots.

The film was given a 12A certificate by the **BBFC**, in common with the other films in the MCU. This was for 'moderate fantasy violence, and injury detail', meaning that no one under the age of 12 can see the film in a cinema, unless accompanied by an adult.

Marketing for the film included:

- A **concept art trailer** revealed at the D23 EXPO (the biennial Official Disney Fan Club three-day event) in August 2015.
- A **teaser trailer** in April 2016.
- Three prelude **tie-in** comics in July, August and September 2016.
- Exclusive clips of the film at **comic-con** events.
- A second **trailer** of the film in July 2016.
- Two 'TV spots' (**trailers** for TV rather than cinema).
- A STEM competition for girls aged 15–18, with a prize to attend the **world premiere**.
- Screening of a 15-minute excerpt in IMAX cinemas in early October 2016.
- **Social media** add-ons, such as Snapchat lenses and Twitter stickers.
- A **sponsorship** deal with Microsoft Surface.
- 3D 'worlds' created by three Google Tilt Brush artists, that could be experienced by the public using VR goggles in New York, London and Hong Kong.

Link

For more on *Doctor Strange* see pages 201–203 of the student book.

One of the *Doctor Strange* comics.

Doctor Strange had its **theatrical** (cinema) **world premiere** on 13 October 2016 in Hong Kong. It had a Hollywood **premiere** on 20 October 2016, and then was **released** simultaneously in 33 countries on 25 October 2016. This included **IMAX release** in 32 of these countries. Altogether, it was **released** on over 1,000 IMAX screens, the largest global **IMAX release** ever. It had been **released** in approximately 80 countries worldwide by January 2017.

Doctor Strange **merchandise** includes: action figures, accessory bags, computer sleeves, phone cases, luggage tags, mugs, water bottles, T-shirts, dart boards, lamps, cushions, bags, socks, magnets, playing cards, badges, beanies, lanyards, wallets, belts, glasses, caps, hoodies and backpacks.

Doctor Strange was also **released** on:

- digital **download** by Walt Disney Studios Home Entertainment (14 February 2017)
- BluRay and DVD (28 February 2017)
- YouTube
- Google Play Movies
- Netflix.

Link

For more on *I, Daniel Blake* see pages 203–204 of the student book.

I, Daniel Blake: *I, Daniel Blake* is a British **social realism** film **directed** by left-wing **film maker** Ken Loach when he was 80 years old. It was his 26th cinema film. *I, Daniel Blake* is about the austerity measures in Britain and what they mean for people who need to rely on benefits. It was **produced** by the independent British company Sixteen Films, along with Why Not Productions and Wild Bunch. The **budget** is undisclosed, but Loach's 2009 film *Looking for Eric* had a **budget** of £4 million. The **funding** came from a range of backers including BBC Films, the BFI and the EU's Creative Europe Fund. *I, Daniel Blake* is a UK/France/Belgium co-production.

Sixteen Films was formed by **director** Ken Loach and **producer** Rebecca O'Brien in 2002. O'Brien has produced most of Loach's films since they worked together on *Hidden Agenda* in 1990.

Filming on *I, Daniel Blake* began in October 2015 in Newcastle upon Tyne, and lasted for five and a half weeks.

The film was given a 15 certificate by the **BBFC**, due to the use of 'very strong language'. This means that no one under the age of 15 can see the film in a cinema.

The film was distributed by eOne. The film's **world premiere** was at Cannes Film Festival on 13 May 2016, where it won the Palme D'Or. It was also shown at over 30 other **film festivals** throughout the world, and was **released** in cinemas in 36 countries, including a **limited release** in the USA and Canada.

eOne's **marketing** for the film included **guerrilla marketing** and **word of mouth**. Five regional marketing managers were employed to work in and with 'grassroots communities', to get people talking about the film before its **release**. The UK **premiere** was held in Newcastle, where the film had been shot, to take it back to its home community. Other **marketing** for the film within the UK included:

Ken Loach with the Palme d'Or he received for *I, Daniel Blake* at the Cannes Film Festival.

- A **trailer**.
- **Screenings** held to coincide with political party conferences.
- Labour Party politicians invited as special guests to the London **premiere**.
- Projecting the film's title and one of its speeches onto the Houses of Parliament.
- Using a high-pressure hose and stencils to create 'clean graffiti' on 200 dirty pavements.
- A **social media** campaign including people reading out the final speech from the film and messages from people affected by the austerity cuts highlighted in the film.
- Hundreds of free **screenings** in UK cinemas several weeks before the film's official **release**.
- A **collaboration** with the *Daily Mirror*, giving away free tickets to its readers, and using the film's graffiti **font** for its **masthead** for a day.
- Loach, O'Brien and the lead actors gave talks at the early **screenings**.
- TV and radio appearances by Loach.

One of the projections on the Houses of Parliament.

Clean graffiti on UK pavements advertising *I, Daniel Blake*.

The film was **released** in the UK in October 2016. It won a BAFTA for Best Picture, along with other awards. The awards helped to boost **public interest** in the film. It has made at least $15.8 million at the **box office** worldwide, making most of this in France and the UK.

Merchandise includes T-shirts, mugs and posters.

I, Daniel Blake was also **released** on:

- BluRay and DVD
- YouTube
- Netflix (but at time of writing not yet in the UK).
- Google Play Movies
- Amazon Prime video

Knowledge Check 7.9

Make a list of the key differences between the ways the two films were produced and distributed that you think were related to their **budgets**.

Doctor Strange	I, Daniel Blake

Answer the following questions about films. Marvel Studios is part of a **conglomerate**. Sixteen Films is an **independent film production** company.

1   Can you find an example of **horizontal integration** in the explanation of the companies involved in the making of *Doctor Strange*?

2   Can you find an example of **vertical integration** in the explanation on page 157 of the companies involved in the making of *Doctor Strange*?

3   How did being part of a **conglomerate** make **production** and distribution of *Doctor Strange* easier to manage than the **production** and **distribution** of *I, Daniel Blake*?

Tip

Your knowledge and understanding of film and the two related CSPs can be assessed in Media One Section B: Industries and Audiences, but any related questions will only focus on Media Industries.

In-depth products: All four areas of the theoretical framework

Newspapers

Rapid Recap

- the *Daily Mirror*
- *The Times*.

For examination in 2019:

- The *Daily Mirror*, Wednesday 15 March 2017, **front page** and pages 4–5, with a focus on the Muirfield story.
- *The Times*, Wednesday 15 March 2017, **front page** and page 17, with a focus on the Muirfield story.

In each case, the selected story needs to be considered within the context of the page on which it is printed.

Daily Mirror CSP pages for examination in 2019

The Times CSP pages for examination in 2019

Muirfield welcomed back to Open after vote allows in women golfers

Alasdair Reid

One of the most acclaimed and prestigious golf courses in Britain is set to host the Open Championship again after its members voted overwhelmingly to end their 273-year-old tradition and allow women to join their club.

Muirfield was dropped from the Open rota last May after a narrow majority of members of the Honourable Company of Edinburgh Golfers, the course owners and the world's oldest golf club, voted against allowing women to join.

The Royal and Ancient (R&A), which runs the Open, responded by declaring that no club with discriminatory membership policies would be allowed to host the tournament.

That move forced a second ballot, which has now overturned the decision, with an 80.2 per cent majority in favour of admitting women.

Within a few minutes of the result being announced yesterday, the R&A confirmed that Muirfield was back on the list of courses they consider suitable as venues for the Open. Muirfield has hosted the tournament 16 times, most recently in 2013, when Phil Mickelson lifted the claret jug. Many top players consider Muirfield to be the best of the Open courses.

"It is extremely important for us in staging one of the world's great sporting events that women can become members at all of our host clubs," said Martin Slumbers, the R&A's chief executive. "Muirfield is a truly outstanding Open venue and we … look forward to taking the championship back there."

The result of the vote was announced by Henry Fairweather, the club captain, who admitted last year that he had been personally embarrassed when the first ballot failed to produce the two-thirds majority required to change the club's constitution. That setback forced modernisers to call a special general meeting, which led to the latest postal ballot and a belated victory for equality.

"This is a significant decision for a club which was founded in 1744 and retains many of the values and aspirations of its founding members," said Mr Fairweather. "We look forward to welcoming women as members who will enjoy, and benefit from, the great traditions and friendly spirit of this remarkable club."

Muirfield is only the latest in a long line of high-profile courses and clubs to come round to the principle of gender equality. Augusta National, which hosts the US Masters, bowed to pressure to admit women in 2012. It was only in 2014 that the R&A itself dropped its controversial men-only policy, with Kent's Royal St George's and Ayrshire's Royal Troon following suit in order to protect their status as open venues.

Aileen Campbell, the Scottish government's minister for sport, said that the decision was encouraging. "This change is extremely positive for equality in Scotland but it's also one that will be beneficial to Muirfield now that the R&A has confirmed the course will be reinstated as an Open venue," she said.

However, Mr Fairweather warned that the club's invitation-only admission procedure suggested that it might be two or three years before they welcomed their first female member.

"Our members had been very clear that they don't want an artificial female presence," he added. "They want them to become members of the club and to be treated equally."

Alyson Rudd, page 60

Gentlemen-only clubs

The Garrick, London
It counts Stephen Fry, Hugh Bonneville and Jeremy Paxman as members. In 2015, members voted to maintain male-only status. Three former Tory MPs and 11 QCs were among those supporting the policy

White's, London
David Cameron, a member for 15 years, resigned in 2008 over the club's refusal to admit women. A notable exception was made for the Queen's visit in 1991 and again in 2016. Members include Prince Charles and the Duke of Cambridge

For examination in 2020:

- The *Daily Mirror*, Saturday 5 May 2018, **front page** and pages 8–9 with a focus on the local election story.
- *The Times*, Saturday 5 May 2018, **front page** and pages 6–7 with a focus on the local election story.

In each case, the selected story needs to be considered within the context of the page on which it is printed.

Daily Mirror CSP pages for examination in 2020

THE TIMES

SATURDAY

Daily newspaper of the year 5 May 2018 | thetimes.co.uk | No 72527 £1 to subscribers £1.90

40 best country house hotels

With stunning walks and bike trails

Weekend

Kay Burley

Don't mess with me

Magazine

Plus Eat! recipe pullout

Magazine

MPs call for inquest as Corbyn fails election test

Labour must 'look at itself' after council setback

Francis Elliott Political Editor
Sam Coates, Lucy Fisher

Royal appointment Sir Paul and Lady McCartney at Buckingham Palace yesterday. He received the insignia of the Companion of Honour, an order limited to 65 members

Continued on page 2, col 3

I've put on a stone in weight! Caitlin Moran

Magazine

Time to fire up the grill Bank holiday barbecue

Weekend

Britain's most

Sam Coates Deputy Political Editor

The Times CSP pages for examination in 2020

Results show that voters want | hard Brexit, ministers tell May

News Local elections

Sam Coates Chief Political Correspondent

Corbyn blamed for loss of Jewish support

Comeback starts here, says Cable after Lib Dem gains

Birmingham remains red despite | scandals

Ukip chief's positive spin: We're like the Black Death

Links

See also:
- Chapter 2 page 36 for the **technical codes** for a **newspaper front page** and **double page spread**.
- Chapter 3 page 73 for a brief discussion of **dominant representations** in the **newspaper** CSPs for 2020.
- Chapter 3 pages 75–76 for an explanation of **news values**.
- Chapter 4 pages 97–98 for **regulation** of the British press.
- Chapter 6 pages 130–131 for sample analysis questions for *The Times* **front page**.
- Chapter 8 pages 196–197 for a sample extended response question focusing on the *Daily Mirror*.

Overall study and contexts of the media

You need to be able to compare and contrast the two **newspaper** CSPs to discover:

- The different **audience demographics** and political and **ideological viewpoints** of the two **newspapers**.
- The role of the press and the arguments for and against **press freedom**.
- The **issues** of **press intrusion**, the ethics and working practices of **newspaper journalists**.
- The political leanings of each **newspaper** and how they are reflected in the content studied.

Media Language

You need to be able to recognise, analyse and discuss:

- The ways in which the **conventions** of **newspapers** – **headlines**, selection of **image**, choice of written **language**, formatting – are used to communicate meaning.
- How choices made in the **construction** of the **front page** and story influence meaning, including creating **narratives**.
- The similarities and differences between the **front pages** and the same stories covered in both **newspapers**.

You need to be able to recognise the different conventions that newspapers use.

Media Representation

You need to be able to recognise, analyse and discuss:

- The **representation** of **social groups**, **issues** or events featured on the **front page** and in the news story.
- How the **selections** made **construct** versions of reality, and convey particular points of view, **messages**, **values** and **beliefs** that reflect the political and **ideological position** of the two **newspapers**.
- How these **selections** direct the **audience** towards particular **interpretations** of the content.

Media Industries

You need to understand and be able to discuss:

- The **market position** of each **newspaper**, including the **circulation** figures and how they have changed.
- The **ownership** of each **newspaper**.
- How the **newspaper** organisations are responding to the challenges to traditional newspapers from **digital platforms**.
- The trends towards **convergence of media platforms**.
- How and why British **newspapers** are **regulated**.

Link

For more on NRS categories see page 91 of the student book.

Media Audiences

You need to understand and be able to discuss:

- The **target audiences** for both **newspapers**, in terms of NRS categories and **demographics**, and a comparison between them.
- How the newspapers attract their **audiences**.
- The pleasures offered to readers of the **newspapers**.
- Whether the **newspapers position** their readers to be active or passive.
- The opportunities offered to **audiences** to negotiate or reject the **preferred reading**.

Contextual and other key information

For **Media Language** and **Media Representations**, most of the key information is held within the CSPs themselves, although some knowledge of the **target audiences** will help you to discuss **Media Representations**. You will not be assessed on your ability to memorise the following information, but you could use your understanding of some of these points in support of a discussion question about **newspaper representations**, industries and/or **audiences**.

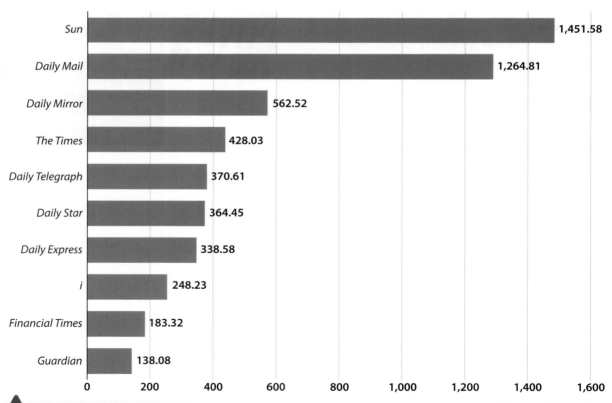

Newspaper	Circulation (thousands)
Sun	1,451.58
Daily Mail	1,264.81
Daily Mirror	562.52
The Times	428.03
Daily Telegraph	370.61
Daily Star	364.45
Daily Express	338.58
i	248.23
Financial Times	183.32
Guardian	138.08

Source: Audit Bureau of Circulations

Circulation in thousands of UK daily newspapers in June 2018

The *Daily Mirror*: The *Daily Mirror* is a **national** daily **tabloid newspaper**, usually supportive of the left wing of British politics. It is part of the **popular** or **downmarket press**, aimed at C1 C2 DEs on the **NRS socio-economic scale**. Its readers anticipate a quick, easy read about what matters to them.

Its **circulation** in June 2018 was 562,520 copies. This was a year-on-year drop of 18%.

The *Daily Mirror/Sunday Mirror/Sunday People*/mirror.co.uk combined **brand reach** (how many people engaged with a product from this group of **newspapers** either in print or online) was 27.1 million people per month in 2017 (Emily Tan (2018) https://www.campaignlive.co.uk/article/pamco-resets-audience-measurement-total-brand-reach-publishers/1462453).

Its **website** is free to access and is **funded** by **advertising**. Digital adverts made up 25% of the **advertising revenue** in 2016, a figure that had risen from 7% since 2012. However, print **advertising** sales were falling throughout that period, so that the Trinity Mirror group was gaining 13 pence of digital **advertising** for every £1 it lost of print **advertising**.

Media ownership can change; so, the following information was accurate in October 2018, but may have changed by the time you read it. The *Daily Mirror* is owned by Reach plc, a British **newspaper**, **magazine** and digital publisher. Reach plc was formerly called Trinity Mirror, until it took over Northern and Shell in February 2018, after which the overall group was renamed. Reach plc also owns the *Sunday Mirror*, *Sunday People*, *Daily Express*, *Daily Star* and *Daily Star Sunday*. These **newspapers** account for a 20% share of **national newspaper circulation**. In addition to these UK national papers, Reach plc also owns Scottish **newspapers** and over 240 regional **newspapers**, as well as the websites associated with these **publications**.

The *Times*: The *Times* is a high status national daily broadsheet newspaper, usually supportive of the right wing of British politics. It is part of the **quality** or **upmarket press**, aimed at ABC1s on the **NRS socio-economic scale**. Its readers anticipate in-depth analysis of important news.

Its **circulation** in June 2018 was 428,030 copies. This was a year-on-year drop of just over 1%.

The combined **brand reach** for *The Times/Sunday Times*/thetimes.co.uk was 8.1 million people per month in 2017.

For more on Reach see page 120 of the student book.

For more on **brand reach** see page 183 of the student book.

Its website has a **paywall** – users can access two articles a week for free, but they have to pay a **subscription** to access any more than this. *The Times* makes a profit from its **website**, and it claimed in July 2018 to have 255,000 **digital** subscribers, slightly more than the number of regular subscribers to its print **newspaper**.

Media ownership can change; so, the following information was accurate in October 2018, but may have changed by the time you read this. *The Times* is published by Times Newspapers, a **subsidiary** of **media conglomerate** News UK, which also own the *Sunday Times, Sun* and *Sun on Sunday*. These four **newspapers** account for about one-third of all paid-for **newspapers** sold in the UK. News UK is **wholly owned** by the **multinational group** News Corp, which owns media and other businesses around the world. News Corp is owned by the Murdoch Family Trust who also currently own 21st Century Fox, although there are advanced plans for the sale of 21st Century Fox to Disney.

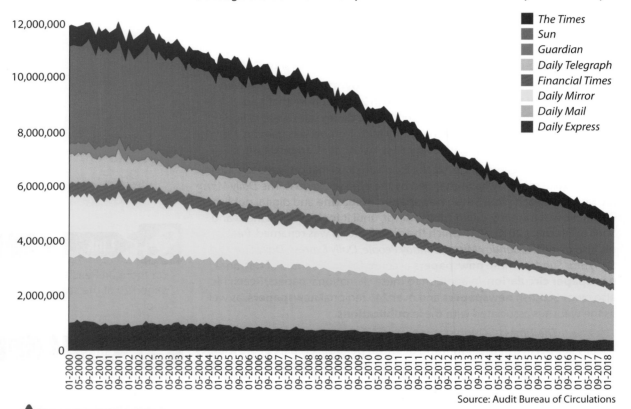

Legend:
- The Times
- Sun
- Guardian
- Daily Telegraph
- Financial Times
- Daily Mirror
- Daily Mail
- Daily Express

Source: Audit Bureau of Circulations

Falling circulation of UK newspapers from 2000 to 2018.

Both **newspapers** have signed up to **regulatory body IPSO** rather than **IMPRESS**. This means they have agreed to follow the Editors' Code of Practice. This covers the following areas:

- accuracy
- privacy
- harassment
- intrusion into shock or grief
- reporting suicide
- children
- children in sex cases
- hospitals
- reporting of crime
- clandestine devices and subterfuge
- victims of sexual assault
- discrimination
- financial journalism
- confidential sources
- witness payments in criminal trials
- payment to criminals
- the **public interest**.

Knowledge Check 7.11

Complete the table to provide a direct comparison between the two **newspapers' front pages** – the first row has been completed for you.

Aspect or element to be analysed	*The Times*		*Daily Mirror*	
	Target audience:		**Target audience:**	
	Sign **What can you see?**	**Connotation** **What does it mean?**	**Sign** **What can you see?**	**Connotation** **What does it mean?**
Number of stories on the **front page**	*Issue for 2020*: one story, six **teasers**	The **newspaper** contains a lot of information	One story, two **teasers**	The **newspaper** is straightforward to read and tells you what is important to know
Content of **images** on the **front page**				
Font style in **masthead**	**Serif font**, all capitals, black			
Font styles in **headlines**			**Sans serif font**, all capitals	
Main **headline**				
Content of **teaser** stories				
Number of paragraphs in lead **front page** story				
Vocabulary within the **headlines** and copy			Familiar and friendly, slang and abbreviations, first names	
Juxtaposition of elements on the page				
Other features such as adverts, price and graphics				

Knowledge Check 7.12

Answer the following questions on your **newspaper** CSPs.

1   What **news values** are exemplified in the **front page** story and focus story in your **newspaper** CSPs?

2   What is the **narrative structure** of the focus story in each **newspaper**? For example:

- What information (**5Ws**) was included in the opening paragraph?
- What (if any) information was included from key witnesses or experts?
- What (if any) pointers were there to the future?
- Looking at the story as a **quest**, what was the main obstacle that needed to be overcome and what was the **prize** to be gained if the **quest** was successful?
- Who or what was the **hero**?
- Who or what was the **villain**?

 Link

For more about **heroes** and **villains** see page 209 of the student book.

Link

For more about **Blumler and Katz's uses and gratifications theory** see page 99 of the student book.

3   How does the **front page** of each **newspaper** meet each of the four categories of **uses and gratifications** in the theory devised by **Blumler and Katz**?

Tip

Your knowledge and understanding of **newspapers** and the two related CSPs can be assessed in either section of Media One and/or in Media Two Section B.

Online, social and participatory media/video games

Spec Spotlight

For this course, online, social and participatory media and video games will be linked. There will be some independent online, social and participatory media products and some independent video games but sometimes these two media forms will be linked and video games will be studied alongside associated online, social and participatory media products.

Rapid Recap

Three sets of products:

- Zoella: **online, social and participatory media**:
    - https://www.zoella.co.uk – **website**
    - https://www.youtube.co.uk/user/zoella280390 – YouTube channel
    - https://twitter.com/zoella – Twitter
    - https://www.instagram.com/zoella – Instagram.
- Kim Kardashian: Hollywood – video game.
- Kim Kardashian: **online, social and participatory media**:
    - https://www.kimkardashianwest.com – **website**
    - https://www.facebook.com/kimkardashian – Facebook
    - https://twitter.com/kimkardashian?lang – Twitter.
- Lara Croft GO (2015) – video game.

Links

See also:

- Chapter 2 page 40 for the **technical codes** of a webpage, page 42 for the **technical codes** of a **vlog** and a video game.
- Chapter 3 page 70 for a question about Kim Kardashian: Hollywood and the **representation** of **social class**.
- Chapter 3 page 74 for a question about Zoella and **dominant representations**.
- Chapter 4 page 99 for information about **regulation** for video games.
- Chapter 5 pages 117–118 for a brief discussion of how Lara Croft GO and Kim Kardashian: Hollywood meet the **audience**'s needs.

Overall study and contexts of the media

You need to be able to compare and contrast the three sets of **online, social and participatory media** and video game CSPs to discover:

- The growing exploitation of **technological developments** in the **media** to create a new generation of online celebrities.
- How the emergence of Kim Kardashian as a cultural phenomenon and of Lara Croft and Zoella as commercial **brands** can be compared: the impact and influence of each one; how they compare as role models; their potential to create powerful messages that contribute to shaping contemporary **values** and **beliefs**; their **cultural influences** on **gender identity** and power.
- How Zoella, Lara Croft and Kim Kardashian reflect the nature of **online participatory audiences** and the link between celebrities and their followers.
- In terms of **gender representation**, whether Lara Croft is an exception or an example of a wider problem in the video game industry.
- The promotion of consumerism, **lifestyle values** and **ideals** alongside discussion of make-up and fashion by Zoella and Kim Kardashian.

Zoella

Media Language

You need to be able to recognise, analyse and discuss:

- The **genre conventions** of each online, social and participatory form that Zoella uses, and how they have become established as **conventions** of this **media form**:
  - the **technical codes** used in Zoella's **vlogs** and the effect they have on the **audience**
  - the **verbal codes** she uses to connect with her **audience**
  - the photographic **images** on her Facebook page and/or Instagram and their **function** in creating Zoella's **brand**
  - the **verbal codes** used in Twitter posts by Zoella and her followers to reveal the nature of the relationship Zoella enjoys with her followers
  - the **narrative structure** of a typical Zoella presentation on her YouTube channel.

Media Representation

You need to be able to recognise, analyse and discuss:

- **Representations** of Zoella herself, people she can be seen with, the products she **endorses** and settings she inhabits.
- The extent to which she embodies and reinforces **gender stereotyping**:
  - how her **representation** is central to the creation of her **brand**
  - whether she trivialises female **gender identity**.

Zoella's YouTube channel was the start of her commercial success.

- How her self-representations portray her interests, concerns, friendships, values and beliefs.
- What sort of critical reception she has had, and how fair the criticisms and positive endorsements are.

Media Industries

You need to understand and be able to discuss:

- The development of Zoella as a commercial **brand**:
  - how she uses her online presence for self-promotion
  - how she has generated a substantial income through her online, social and participatory forms
  - who she has formed collaborations with and the benefits for her commercial partners in this move away from more traditional forms of **marketing** and promotion.
- The implications for **traditional media industries** of the success of online vloggers such as Zoella.

Media Audiences

You need to understand and be able to discuss:

- The **demographics** and **psychographics** of Zoella's **target audience**.
- Why she has proven to be so popular with them – the nature of her appeal.
- Evidence within the CSP products of specific **audience targeting**.
- The opportunities for **audience participation** across Zoella's online products.
- The types of pleasure, **uses and gratifications** that are available for the intended **audience** of these products.
- The extent of Zoella's influence on her **target audience**.
- The potential to generate **oppositional readings**.

Contextual and other key information

For **Media Language** and **Media Representations**, most of the key information is held within the CSPs themselves, although some knowledge of the **target audiences** will help you to discuss **Media Representations**. You will not be assessed on your ability to memorise the following information, but you could use your understanding of some of these points in support of a discussion question about **online, social and participatory media** and video game **representations**, industries and/or **audiences**.

Zoella is the name of the fashion, beauty and **lifestyle vlog** created by Zoe Sugg in 2009 and posted on YouTube. The **vlog** has been hugely successful with **audiences**, as has her **social media profile** on other online and social participatory forms. She is one of the new generation of online vloggers and the success of Zoella has enabled Sugg to branch into a range of other forms of **merchandising**, increasing the scope of the potential influence she has over her **target audience**. She has built a consistent **brand** across a range of **social media platforms** and of commercial products aimed at her **target audience**, such as novels, make-up, accessories and, famously, an advent calendar (see 'Boots Cuts Price of Zoella's £50 12-Door Advent Calendar in Half After YouTube Star Faces Heavy Criticism', *Independent*, https://www. independent.co.uk/life-style/gadgets-and-tech/boots-zoella-advent-calender-price-cut-half-12-door-youtube-star-fans-criticism-a8056006.html).

All of Zoella's OSP **media products** are free to access. Zoella's YouTube channel has 12 million subscribers. She has 13 million followers on Twitter, 2.5 million on Facebook and 10.6 million on Instagram. Her YouTube videos collectively get about 22 million clicks a month. These videos give her an annual income of £180,000. Some of her videos are financially sponsored by brands such as Daniel Wellington and Boohoo, which brings in further income. A single promotional post on Instagram could earn Zoella £12,000. She also gets income from sales of her books and cosmetics. Her estimated net worth is £2.5 million.

Social **media** channels are **regulated** by their 'rules of use' – a form of **self-regulation**. **Platform providers** such as YouTube and Facebook use computer algorithms to detect offensive or inappropriate material, as well as responding to **audience** reports of such material. Increasingly, they are also employing teams of people to check the content posted by users on their **platforms**, in response to pressure from the public, big businesses and governments around the world.

As well as the **uses and gratifications** mentioned in the theories of **Blumler and Katz**, Zoella's output also offers other pleasures, such as the **voyeuristic pleasure** of watching the lives of others and of knowing 'secrets' about the intimate life of a celebrity.

Kim Kardashian

Media Language

You need to be able to recognise, analyse and discuss:

- How **narrative ingredients** are used in the game such as **character types**, **settings** and events.
  - the types of characters we meet, where are they and what are they doing
  - how the **gameplay** drives the **narrative** and how the player impacts on the action.
- The **visual appeal** of the game.
- How the choice of elements in Kim Kardashian: Hollywood **represents** the world in a way that puts over **messages** and **values**.

Screengrab from the **video game** Kim Kardashian: Hollywood

Media Representation

You need to be able to recognise, analyse and discuss:

- **Representations** of **femininity** and **masculinity**, **place**, **social class**, **ethnicity** and **age** in the game.
- To what extent Kardashian has been able to control her **representation** in the game.
- **Stereotypes** featured in the game and how they appeal to the **target audience**.
- How the use of **representation** can encourage **audiences** to aspire to a particular type of lifestyle or to adopt a particular type of appearance.
- The **social groups** not represented.
- A feminist approach to the **representations** in the game.

Media Industries

You need to understand and be able to discuss:

- The effect the **institution** responsible for Kim Kardashian: Hollywood had on the product.
- How the game and Kim Kardashian's online presence demonstrate **convergence**.
- How video games such as Kim Kardashian: Hollywood are **regulated** and **rated**.
- Whether Kim Kardashian: Hollywood has been commercially successful.
- What Kim Kardashian: Hollywood tells us about the ways in which the video game industry is changing and developing.

Media Audiences

You need to understand and be able to discuss:

- How the **demographics** of game-players have shifted away from the dominance of male players.
- The **target audience** for this video game.
- The types of pleasures playing the game offers them.
- Whether the **uses and gratifications theory** is helpful in understanding the appeal of this game.
- The types of influence this product might have on **audiences**, including the negative influence on **audiences** pointed to by critics of gaming.
- The material used to **advertise** and **market** the game and what it says about the intended **audience**.

Contextual and other key information

For **Media Language** and **Media Representations**, most of the key information is held within the CSPs themselves, although some knowledge of the **target audiences** will help you to discuss **Media Representations**. You will not be assessed on your ability to memorise the following information, but you could use your understanding of some of these points in support of a discussion question about **online, social and participatory media** and video game **representations**, industries and/or **audiences**.

The goal of this **turn-based** video game is to increase your fame and reputation by working your way up to join an A list of celebrity status. It epitomises our society's interest in fame and celebrity. The **narrative** of the game also reflects our consumerist **culture** and, along with the other online platforms that Kardashian uses, demonstrates how **technological developments** in the **media** are being exploited by famous people for commercial gain and to increase their public profile.

Kim Kardashian: Hollywood is a **freemium game** app for mobile phones, tablets and PCs. **In-app purchases** are available and actively encouraged within the **gameplay**. There is also **advertising** within the game itself.

Kim Kardashian: Hollywood was developed by Glu Games Inc., and was first available for **download** in June 2014. Within a month of its **release**, it was one of the top five games on the iOS App Store. The game has generated over $200 million of income through **in-app purchases**, **sponsorship** and **advertising** deals. Kim Kardashian occasionally posts tweets about the game, and also advises on which of the outfits she has recently been shown wearing on **social media** should appear in the game. There is **synergy** between the game and her **social media output**.

PEGI provides **age ratings** for **boxed games**. **Downloadable** free-to-play games are rated either by **PEGI** for Stream and GooglePlay, or by the **app store** for Android and iOS. Kim Kardashian: Hollywood has an **age rating** of 12+ on the iTunes store. This is for:

- infrequent/mild sexual content and nudity
- infrequent/mild mature/suggestive **themes**
- infrequent/mild alcohol, tobacco, or drug use or references
- infrequent/mild horror/fear **themes**
- infrequent/mild cartoon or fantasy violence
- infrequent/mild profanity or crude humour.

Kim Kardashian: Hollywood builds on Kim Kardashian's personal **brand** as a celebrity, as well as the pre-existing **brand** of the Kardashian family. It has been said that they are 'famous for being famous', and the game builds on this notion.

As well as the **uses and gratifications** mentioned in the theories of **Blumler and Katz**, Kim Kardashian: Hollywood also offers other pleasures, such as the **visceral pleasure** of overcoming adversaries, the **vicarious pleasure** of living your life through your **avatar** and the **catharsis** enabled by succeeding in a particular task.

Link

For more on PEGI **age ratings** see page 148 of the student book.

Lara Croft GO

Media Language

Screengrab from the video game Lara Croft GO

You need to be able to recognise, analyse and discuss:

- The **narrative features** of Lara Croft GO such as character, **setting**, **narrative conflicts** and their **resolution**.
- The division between the traditional heroic figure (Lara Croft) and the opponents she encounters during the course of the game.
- The use of clear elements of the **action adventure genre** within a **turn-based** puzzle game.
- The **connotations** of various elements including Lara Croft's appearance, the music and game **settings**.
- Any elements of **intertextuality**.
- The **visual appeal** of the game.

Media Representation

You need to be able to recognise, analyse and discuss:

- The **representation** of Lara Croft herself as the central **protagonist** in the game.
- The extent to which she **conforms** to or **subverts** the **stereotype** of the female role and identity:
  - her appearance and behaviour in the game
  - whether she adopts characteristics of **masculine gender identity**.
- The type of **audiences** she appeals to.
- The use of other **game elements**, including the ways in which good and evil are represented.
- **Representations** of time and place.

Media Industries

You need to understand and be able to discuss:

- The company responsible for **developing** and **publishing** the game.
- The game as part of a larger **franchise** – what advantages a **franchise** offers to the game's **producers**.
- Whether Lara Croft GO has been commercially successful.
- How the availability of the game across a variety of **devices** contributes to its success.
- How video games are **rated** and **regulated**.

Media Audiences

You need to understand and be able to discuss:

- The **target audience** for this video game.
- The types of pleasures offered by playing the game.
- How games such as Lara Croft GO fulfil **audience** needs and **desires**.
- The types of influence this product might have on **audiences**, including the negative influence on **audiences** pointed to by critics of gaming.
- The material used to **advertise** and **market** the game and what it says about the **intended audience**.
- Reviews of the game.

Contextual and other key information

For **Media Language** and **Media Representations**, most of the key information is held within the CSPs themselves, although some knowledge of the **target audiences** will help you to discuss **Media Representations**. You will not be assessed on your ability to memorise the following information, but you could use your understanding of some of these points in support of a discussion question about **online, social and participatory media** and video game representations, industries and/or **audiences**.

Lara Croft GO forms part of the Tomb Raider video games **franchise**. Since its first launch in 1996, the **franchise** has enjoyed phenomenal global success. As a game character, Lara Croft has polarised opinions: some viewing her as a positive female **role model**, while others are critical of her appearance. There are strongly contrasting views of the perceived quality of the Tomb Raider games. However, there can be no doubt of the commercial success of the **franchise**. Lara Croft's success transcends many **media forms** and **platforms** including big-**budget** Hollywood films, comic books and novels.

Lara Croft GO is a **premium** (paid-for) **game app** for mobile phones, tablets and PCs, costing £4.99 usually, but with special offer reductions to 99p at times. Players' progress is saved online so they can pick up the game as they swap from one **platform** to another. Players can choose which costume Lara Croft wears, but these have no impact on **gameplay**. New outfits can be paid for or unlocked by completing certain **levels** of the game.

Lara Croft GO was developed by Square Enix Montreal, as the second in their GO series of **premium mobile games**, and first went on sale in August 2015. It was Apple's iOS game of the year for 2015. In February 2018, Square Enix said it wouldn't develop any more GO games, as, despite 'great **revenue**' since Lara Croft GO was developed, the **premium mobile game** market was decreasing as **audiences** know they can now **download** thousands of games for free.

Lara Croft GO has a **PEGI age rating** of 7+. This is due to non-realistic looking violence towards fantasy characters, and pictures or sounds likely to be scary to young children.

The Tomb Raider **brand** was originally developed by the British company Eidos Interactive. This company was taken over by Japanese video game developers Square Enix in 2009. Square Enix itself was formed by the **merger** of Square and Enix in 2003. Since then it has **acquired** a number of other companies, and created new **subsidiaries**, thus becoming a **conglomerate**. In 2018, it had **subsidiaries** based in Japan, the USA, China, the UK and Canada, and provides an example of **media** industry **globalisation**.

The game is very much part of the Tomb Raider **brand**, showing the **protagonist** Lara Croft gathering artefacts in underground labyrinths, and being pitted against creatures that are set to stop her. However, it also brings in new elements by being a puzzle-based game rather than an **action adventure game**. This allows it to attract a new **audience** to the overall **brand**, as well as potentially attracting a pre-existing **audience** to a new **genre** of game.

Statistics from 2017 and 2018 show that women make up 49% of all **mobile gamers**, but they play more frequently than male **mobile gamers**. They prefer games that can be played on their **smartphones** in short bursts wherever they are; they play fewer unique games; they spend less money on the games and in-game; and prefer games that feature female characters.

As well as the **uses and gratifications** mentioned in the theories of **Blumler and Katz**, Lara Croft GO also offers other pleasures, such as the **aesthetic pleasure** of well-designed scenarios, the **visceral pleasure** of overcoming adversaries, the **cerebral pleasure** of overcoming the puzzles in the game and the **catharsis** enabled by succeeding at a particular task.

Tip

Your knowledge and understanding of **online, social and participatory media** and video games, and the three related sets of CSPs, can be assessed in either section of Media One and/or in Media Two Section B.

Complete the following table about the **narrative** of the two video game CSPs.

Questions about the quest narrative	Kim Kardashian: Hollywood	Lara Croft GO
Who is the **hero**, despatched on the **quest**?		
What is the goal of the **quest**?		
Who is the **despatcher** sending the **hero** on the **quest**?		
What obstacles does the **hero** encounter?		
Who or what are the **antagonists**?		
Who or what is the **donor**, giving advice or powers?		
What is the **prize** if the **quest** is successful?		
Give an example of an **enigma** in the game and its solution.		
Give an example of a **binary opposite** in the game.		

Knowledge Check 7.14

Answer the following questions on your video game CSPs.

1 How do the three characters of Zoella, Kim Kardashian and Lara Croft provide different **representations** of **femininity**?

2 Who has been involved in the **mediation** of each **representation**?

3 How can the **audience** for each product **interact** with the product and/or its producers?

4 How does each product satisfy the four main types of **uses and gratifications**, according to the theories of **Blumler and Katz**:
- **entertainment and diversion**
- information and education
- **social interaction**
- **personal identity**?

Television

Rapid Recap

Two products:

- *Class* (2016) BBC TV series. Episode 4: 'Co-Owner of a Lonely Heart'
- *Doctor Who* (1963) BBC TV series. Episode 1: 'An Unearthly Child'.

Doctor Who: 'An Unearthly Child' | *Class*: 'Co-Owner of a Lonely Heart'

Link 🔗

See also Chapter 5 page 184 for a brief discussion of the **historical context** of *Doctor Who*'s first episode.

Overall study and contexts of the media

You need to be able to compare and contrast the two television CSPs to discover:

- Changing **representations** of **social groups**: how the two products reflect **society** and **culture** at the times of their **production** in different **historical contexts**.
- *Doctor Who* as an enduring cultural phenomenon.
- The similarities and differences between these **media products** in terms of when they were produced.
- The development of **genre conventions** and the impact of **new technologies** on the **production process**.

Media Language

You need to be able to recognise, analyse and discuss:

- How codes and **conventions** are used to communicate **meaning** in both TV episodes
- The **genre** of the two series as is demonstrated by the CSP episodes, including any elements of **hybridity** or **intertextuality**.
- The **narrative structure**.
- How useful **narrative theories** (such as **Propp**) are in the analysis and understanding of this product.

Media Representation

You need to be able to recognise, analyse and discuss:

- **Representations** of place, education, **masculinity** and **femininity**, **social class** and **age** in both CSPs, and of **heterosexuality** and **homosexuality**, **ethnicity**, ability and disability in *Class*.
- **Representations** of the world through **constructions of reality** within a fantasy theme.
- **Stereotypes** and their **functions**.
- The **social**, **cultural** and **political significance** of **representations** or the absence of **representation** of some **social groups** in relation to the aims of the **producers**, **target audience** and **historical context** in which the series was produced.

Media Industries

You need to understand and be able to discuss:

- The role of the BBC as a **public service broadcaster** in the 1960s.
- The role of BBC Three within the BBC as a whole and the broader **issues** arising from the **convergence** of broadcast and online platforms for television.
- The similarities and differences between 'An Unearthly Child' and 'Co-Owner of a Lonely Heart' in terms of **production processes** and **technologies**.
- The difference between the television **environment** of the early 1960s and today's multi-channel, multi-platform TV landscape.
- How programmes such as *Class* are **funded** and **commissioned**.
- How important the *Doctor Who* **franchise** has been for the BBC, including its sale to other countries.
- How television programmes are **regulated** on different **platforms** (e.g. broadcast, on-demand and video).

Media Audiences

You need to understand and be able to discuss:

- The **target audience** for both products.
- The critical reception of both products and the size of their **audiences**, including how *Doctor Who* fans reacted to *Class*.
- How the **target audience** affected the **marketing** and distribution of *Class*.
- Any evidence of specific **audience targeting** in *Class* Episode 4.
- The **narrative techniques** used to engage the **audience** in *Doctor Who* Episode 1.
- The pleasures, uses and gratifications available to today's **audience** of both products.
- How contemporary **audiences** may interpret *Doctor Who* differently from the original **audience** in the 1960s.
- The factors that influence whether or not **audiences** accept or reject the **preferred readings** of these shows.

Contextual and other key information

For **Media Language** and **Media Representations**, most of the key information is held within the CSPs themselves, although some knowledge of the **target audiences** will help you to discuss **Media Representations**. You will not be assessed on your ability to memorise the following information, but you could use your understanding of some of these points in support of a discussion question about television **representations**, industries and/or **audiences**.

Doctor Who: 'An Unearthly Child': *Doctor Who*: 'An Unearthly Child' was the first ever episode of *Doctor Who*, a **science fiction** series broadcast in 1963 on the BBC. At that time, there were only two television **channels** in the UK – BBC TV and ITV. BBC Two was launched the following year. At the time of the episode's broadcast, ITV had been established for eight years. *Doctor Who* was one attempt by the BBC to compete with commercial **television**, which could command bigger **budgets**. The series was **commissioned** by BBC's head of drama, Sydney Newman, who was recruited from ITV, where he had overseen the introduction of another successful sci-fi series, often known as the *Pathfinders* series and including the original **serial** *Target Luna*.

William Hartnell played the role of the Doctor and was to become the first of 13 re-generations of this character, so far.

The BBC was formed in 1927, with John Reith as its first Director-General. He set up its **guiding principles**, which were written into its **Charter**. It was to be a **public service broadcasting (PSB)** organisation, receiving its finance from the **licence fee**. It could carry no commercials, but would also not be subject to government interference as long as it kept to its **Charter**. BBC programmes should be **unbiased**, uphold morality, and set out to *'educate, inform and entertain'* (BBC, Inside the BBC, https://www.bbc.co.uk/corporate2/insidethebbc/whoweare/mission_and_values).

The first episode of *Doctor Who* was made at the height of the Cold War – when the USSR and the USA (along with their allies) were taking up hostile positions towards each other. People were afraid of impending nuclear war. Competition between these two nations spilled over into the 'Space Race' as each tried to be the first country to conquer new territories beyond the Earth. The USSR launched the first manned space flight in April 1961. The first moon-landing, achieved by the Americans, didn't happen until July 1969. *Doctor Who* was **commissioned** between these two events, when interest in what was 'out there' was particularly high.

This was the first episode of a 42-episode **season**, which contained eight separate **serials**. The episode 'An Unearthly Child' was the first part of a four-part **serial**, with the **serial** also usually referred to as *An Unearthly Child*. Its **target audience** was 'the family' including fairly young children. With only two channels, and only one television in a household, families tended to watch together. The first episode was viewed by 4.4 million people in the UK, with the highest **viewing figure** for that **serial** being 6.9 million for Episode 3. The highest **viewing figure** for the **season** was 10.4 million, with five episodes hitting this height.

Cameras at the time were heavy and inflexible, and film was shot in black and white. They had limited ability to move, and the whole episode had to be shot on indoor **sets**. Many **TV drama** shows were performed live, but *Doctor Who* was recorded 'live to videotape' and then broadcast later. Because of the limited ability to move the camera or the actors very far, the **narrative** was carried by dialogue more than by action.

Although an **age rating** certificate is not required for TV broadcast, it is required for DVD sales. For this purpose, 'An Unearthly Child' has been rated PG.

Class: 'Co-Owner of a Lonely Heart': *Class*: 'Co-Owner of a Lonely Heart' is Episode 4 of an eight-episode teen drama/fantasy/sci-fi **hybrid** genre series that was originally created for the **online television channel** BBC Three and later shown on BBC One. At the time of writing, the series is still available to watch on BBC iPlayer. BBC Three had been a **terrestrial broadcast channel**, but was moved to online only to cut costs, as its **niche** young adult **audience** was moving away from broadcast television towards the **internet** and **streaming services**. As an online-only programme when shown on BBC Three, *Class* was more likely to be viewed by people watching alone than with families or friends. *Class* was also aired on BBC America.

Due to disappointing **audience** figures, no second series was **commissioned**. The BBC does not need to make money from selling **advertising time**, but it does need good **audience** figures to justify the **licence fee**, showing that it is fulfilling its role as a **public service broadcaster**.

The cameras used for the first *Doctor Who* episode were large and heavy.

Class is one of several **spin-offs** from *Doctor Who* over the past few years. Others include *Torchwood* (2006–2011) and the *Sarah Jane Adventures* (2007–2011). Each **spin-off** series has **targeted** a different **audience**. *Torchwood* was for adults, broadcast post-**watershed**. *Sarah Jane Adventures* was for children and was shown on CBBC. *Class* was aimed at the young adult **market** and was shown on BBC Three. The series was set in the same school, Coal Hill, as the original *Doctor Who* episode. As a programme aimed at young adults, *Class* focuses on group and personal relationships, and has a **cast** of teenage characters, with much greater diversity than the original *Doctor Who* series. The audience is **positioned** to **identify** with these young characters.

Although an **age rating** certificate is not required for TV broadcast, it is required for DVD sales. For this purpose, the series of *Class* has been rated 15, but your CSP episode has been rated 12.

Technical equipment has progressed a lot since 1963, and *Class* was able to benefit from the ease of outdoor shooting, as well as the use of **crane shots**, **point-of-view (POV)** shots, and **whip pans**. The episode begins with a **cold opening pre-title sequence** that throws the **audience** into the middle of the action, with the episode's **equilibrium** coming later in the programme. This has become an acceptable **convention** of **TV drama**, understood by contemporary **audiences**.

Audience pleasures from the episode include **visceral pleasure** in the action **scenes**, and **cerebral pleasure** from working out the complicated plot and set of **enigmas**.

Tip

Your knowledge and understanding of television and the two related CSPs will be assessed in Media Two Section A.

Knowledge Check 7.15

1   How do the characters of Susan and April provide different **representations** of teenagers?

(Continued on next page)

2 How do the **representations** of teachers differ between the two television CSPs?

3 How has each **representation** been **mediated**?

4 How does each product satisfy the four main types of **uses and gratifications**, according to the theories of **Blumler and Katz**:
- **entertainment and diversion**
- **social interaction**
- information and education
- **personal identity**?

5 How and why would an **audience** now interpret the *Doctor Who* episode differently from an audience in 1963?

6 What part does the **sequence** between the title *Doctor Who* and the episode title, serve in the **narrative** of the episode?

Knowledge Check 7.16

Complete the following table about the **narrative** of the two television CSPs.

Questions about the quest narrative	*Doctor Who*: 'An Unearthly Child'	*Class*: 'Co-Owner of a Lonely Heart'
Who is the **hero**, despatched on the **quest**?		
What is the goal of the **quest**?		
Who is the **despatcher** sending the **hero** on the **quest**?		
What obstacles does the **hero** encounter?		
Who or what are the **antagonists**?		
Who or what is the **donor**, giving advice or powers?		
What is the **prize** if the **quest** is successful?		
Give an example of an **enigma** in the episode and its solution.		
Give an example of a **binary opposite** in the episode.		

Check It

1 Give two cover lines from *Tatler*'s front cover that imply a target audience in the AB socio-economic range.

2 Why is the price on the *Reveal* front cover in such a large point size?

3 What is the target audience for *Reveal*?

4 What is the denotation of the woman's actions on the OMO print advert?

5 Who was Audrey Hepburn?

6 How was Audrey Hepburn involved in the Galaxy TV advert?

7 Why was Lady Leshurr chosen to front the NHS Blood and Transplant online video?

8 When was Radio 1 launched?

9 How is the BBC financed?

10 Define the term 'public service broadcaster'.

11 Why was Julie Adenuga chosen as a presenter for Beats 1 Radio?

12 How can Apple benefit from having its own global radio station?

13 Explain how Arctic Monkeys and One Direction grew their original fanbase.

14 Which record labels were the two bands signed to when they made the two music video CSPs?

15 Define the term 'blockbuster'.

16 Which conglomerate is Marvel a part of?

17 What is the name of Ken Loach's film production company?

18 What was Loach's role in relation to the film *I, Daniel Blake*?

19 Which has the larger audience, the *Daily Mirror* or *The Times*?

20 What does 'the public interest' mean?

21 Which organisation owns *The Times*?

22 What is a paywall on a website?

23 List at least three of the uses and gratifications in Blumler and Katz's theory.

24 What does celebrity endorsement mean?

25 Which company developed Kim Kardashian: Hollywood?

26 Which company developed Lara Croft GO?

27 What is the age rating of each of these games?

28 When was the BBC established?

29 What was the original target audience for *Doctor Who*?

30 How did this differ from the target audience for *Class*?

8 Exam practice and techniques

Exam techniques and preparing for exams

There is no preferred blueprint or outline plan for answering any of the questions on the two papers. The number of points you need to cover, or the formats of your essays, are not mentioned in the marking criteria.

What is most important is that you *know* the information and skills you have been taught, and can *apply* these to the questions that are set.

You will need to know the four areas of the *theoretical framework* – **Media Language**, **Media Representations**, **Media Industries** and **Media Audiences** – and all the CSPs. In looking at these products during your GCSE Media Studies course you will also have covered different **media contexts**.

Look at sample or past papers

You will probably feel less stressed as you head into the exam room if you are familiar with the overall style and **layout** of the exam papers. The first papers will be taken in 2019, so there will be no past papers before this, but sample papers have been available since 2017 on the AQA website, under GCSE Media Studies. Past papers are usually available on the AQA website from about a year after they have been taken by students. Your teacher will have access to past papers earlier than this.

Make sure you look at some sample or past papers when you are preparing for the exam. You will see how the questions are laid out and how much space you are given for the answers.

The **unseen sources** and print extracts from CSPs are not always allowed to be included in the exam papers online, for copyright reasons. If this is the case, there will be a link or an explanation on the paper. Rest assured that in the real exam you will have a good quality version of any products you are asked to look at, in full-colour.

Mark schemes can be **downloaded** from the same webpage for any papers that have been posted there. You can use these to see what the examiners were looking for and how they are going to be marking *your* answers. For the sample papers, there is a lot of 'indicative content' in the mark schemes. These are aspects that the examiners think students might write about in response to the set question. Remember that the analysis questions are

often open-ended, giving you choice about which aspects you want to write about. For this reason, there is much more here than any individual student would be expected to write. Even so, there could be students (including you) who select specific details to analyse that are not in the indicative content. If these details are just as relevant to the question, the examiners will mark them in the same way, according to the set criteria.

Revise your Close Study Products

Make sure you know all of your products in relation to the relevant areas of the *theoretical framework*. You could create a table such as the one below, filling in the names of your CSPs. This will help you to remember what to revise for each of the CSPs, and you can use this as a checklist to ensure you cover all of them during your revision period.

Media form	Your CSPs	Paper One: language and representations	Paper One: audiences and industries	Paper Two: all four areas
Magazines	e.g. *Tatler*	✓		
Advertising and marketing		✓		
Newspapers		✓	✓	✓
Online, social and participatory media		✓	✓	✓
Video games		✓	✓	✓
Radio			✓	
Music video			✓	
Film			✓*	
Television				✓

*****Media Industries** only

Practise your analysis: unseen source

As you are already aware that there will be at least one unseen product in Paper One, you should practise analysing products in print form. Try to think of as many possibilities as you can, such as:

- print adverts
- webpages
- **magazine** and **newspaper** pages
- screenshots from films and tv programmes
- **screengrabs** from video games
- video game covers.

You are surrounded by such products every day – you can practise this skill almost anywhere and at any time. Remember that your practice analyses only need to focus on **Media Language** and **Media Representations**.

Knowledge Check 8.1

no one should have no one at Christmas

No one to hang the tinsel with.
Or mistletoe for that matter.
No one to share a sherry, a gift or a cracker.
No one to say Happy Christmas to.
Or bring you mince pies in bed.
No one to make one day any different from the rest.
No one, but no one, should have no one at Christmas.

Will you send a text to help provide companionship, advice and support for a lonely older person?

TEXT CHRISTMAS to 70111 to give £3 and help answer a call to the Age UK Advice Line

ageUK
Love later life

Print advert for Age UK

Choose one product, such as the Christmas print advert for Age UK shown left. Analyse the product to see how its different elements communicate meaning.

- Make notes on the **denotations** and **connotations** in the product.
- Remember to look at all aspects of the **mise-en-scène**, as well as the copy (if any): **vocabulary**, **fonts**, colours, size and positioning.
- Look at the **juxtaposition** of the different elements within the product.
- Look for the use of **stereotypes** and consider why these have been used.
- You could also see how **Propp**'s narrative theory could be applied.

If you know the **historical, cultural, social** or **political context** for a product, consider how this has influenced the **representations** within the product. In the advert above, for example, how has the time of year affected the **representations**?

Tip

The more often you carry out analyses like this, the more familiar the process will be when you are in the exam.

Practise your analysis: television CSPs

In the Media Two exam, you will be shown an extract from one of your television CSPs that is approximately three minutes long. You will have to analyse it in response to at least one specific question. For example, you may be asked about aspects such as **genre**, **narrative** or the **representation** of **social groups** or **issues**.

You will already have studied the whole episode, so will be familiar with the overall **narrative**, **mise-en-scène** and characters. You will have analysed many aspects of the episode in class. Make sure you answer the exam questions in relation to the clip you have been shown in the exam. You will not gain marks on these questions for answering about the CSP as a whole, if they specify the extract.

Although you can practise this using your CSP products, you can also practise some of the skills by using a three-minute extract from any TV programme or other video you know well. The key skill you are rehearsing here is focusing your writing on a specific question about the specific extract you have seen.

Remember that in the exam you will watch the extract twice and will have time to make notes from your viewings. You will have looked at the questions about the clip before you view the extract, so will know what to make notes on. Practise this part of the process as well.

On the first viewing, even though you already know the episode, you should aim to watch and listen to as much of the clip as possible, while thinking about the questions. This means you should probably only note down key words, spaced well apart on your paper, to remind you of the most important things you have noticed. In the five-minute break between screenings, you can then expand on these key words. You might find that *you* now have specific questions that you want to check on during the second viewing, such as what exactly a character said, how someone else reacted, or at what point a certain detail was revealed. Make sure to check for these during the second viewing.

You could analyse a sequence from a programme you watched as a child, such as the CBBC show, *Young Dracula*.

Knowledge Check 8.2

Choose a video you know well, such as a TV show you watched as a child. Watch the first three minutes of an episode, and make notes on the following sample exam question: Explain how age* is represented in the extract.

*Instead of 'age' in this question, you could use other aspects such as 'place', **'social class'** or **'gender'**.

Read the questions carefully

Many of the questions will require your analysis or your response to a 'debate' style of question. In these cases, there are going to be many different ways to answer the question. Your response needs to be relevant, well-argued and should use specific, detailed evidence from the required CSP or **unseen source**. Key to providing a good answer will be that you have read the question properly and made sure that you are answering the question that has been set. It can be tempting to try to write everything you know about a CSP, but some of this information will not be relevant, and will get in the way of you showing what you do know about the issue in the question.

> You could be asked to analyse a webpage, such as this one from the Tomb Raider Movie website, as an unseen source.

For example, in Media One Section A, as you have seen, you will be asked questions about an **unseen source**, and about the CSPs related to **Language** and **Representations**. You will be asked specifically to *analyse* some of these products. Questions such as this will usually ask you to analyse the product in relation to something, such as **narrative theory**, **representations** of **gender** or the ability to communicate meaning. You are being asked to write about the product in detail, exploring how individual elements of **Media Language** work together to create a specific meaning or effect on the **audience**, **construct** a specific **representation**, or perhaps create a specific appeal. This means that you need to discuss **connotations** rather than simply **denotations**.

Knowledge Check 8.3

Sample exam question:

> Analyse the 'Story' page from the Tomb Raider Movie website, to show how gender is represented in the Lara Croft character.

Which of these sentences about the **images** on the webpage feature *analysis* that is *relevant* to the question?

	Relevant	Not relevant
1 The webpage has a main image and two smaller images, with the main image being on the left.	☐	☐
2 The three images all show Lara Croft in different action situations, including using weapons such as a bow and arrow.	☐	☐
3 She is physically attractive, and has a skimpy vest top, which helps to make her attractive to the heterosexual male audience.	☐	☐
4 However, she is shown to be active and strong, rather than fitting the 'damsel in distress' stereotype, so female audience members might be drawn to the film because they want to be like her.	☐	☐
5 The images are obviously set somewhere hot, connoted by the sunlight and the way she is dressed.	☐	☐
6 Lara Croft is always looking slightly to one side of the camera, rather than straight at the audience, so there is no direct mode of address.	☐	☐

Other long-answer questions could ask 'how' or 'why' or could ask you to 'explain'. Make sure you understand what you are being asked to do.

Some questions will give you a statement and ask you to debate this. Such questions could use phrases such as 'To what extent … ?', 'How far do you agree with this statement/view?' or 'How far is this shown to be true?' You are being asked for your opinion, but you must show that your opinion is based on evidence from **media products** or **media industries** and **audiences**. Make sure you read the statement carefully, and consider what you can draw from the named CSPs, or from the **unseen source** with the question, that is relevant to that statement. These are *debate* questions and, as discussed earlier in this chapter, you can choose to agree or disagree with the statement. Strong answers will often examine arguments on both sides before deciding that one side is probably *more* correct than the other.

Finally, if you are told in a question that 'you must refer to …' or 'your answer should refer to …' a specific CSP or to a list of bullet points, make sure you do exactly that – there will be specific marks for doing this.

Extended response questions and the synoptic question

There will be one extended response question on Media One – worth 20 marks. This question will give you some bullet points to guide you as to what to include, including which of your CSPs you should refer to, and which of the contexts you need to write about. You should aim to write about each of the bullet points somewhere in your answer, but you don't have to cover them all equally.

Media Two will also have extended response questions, including the **synoptic question**. Remember to read these questions carefully, ensuring that you answer everything asked, and that you refer to the correct CSPs or the correct aspects of the extract.

On the front of the Media Two paper, the **synoptic question** will be clearly sign-posted, with wording such as:

> Question z is a synoptic question in which you should draw together knowledge and understanding from across your full course of study.

The wording at the start of the question will say something like:

> In this question you will be rewarded for drawing together knowledge and understanding from across your full course of study, including different areas of the theoretical framework and media contexts.

This indicates that you will be asked about an issue where you will be able to apply more than one of the four areas of the **theoretical framework**. For example, you may be asked to relate the **media language** and **media representations** used within a given product to the **media industries** that produced it or the **audiences** that engage with that product. You might use what you have learned about the **target audience** for one of your CSPs to explain why certain people or characters have been represented as they are.

Some of your CSPs come from different contexts, so you might be asked to explain how the contexts have had an impact on the products – how an industry, its products or its **audiences** have changed over time, for example.

Here is an example of a potential **synoptic question**:

> 'The growth of the internet has caused other, more traditional, media forms to change in order to survive.' How far is this true of the *Daily Mirror* (CSP)?
>
> *In this question you will be rewarded for drawing together knowledge and understanding from across your full course of study, including different areas of the theoretical framework and media contexts.*

Remember that this is an extended response question and, as was shown earlier, this means you will be assessed on the quality of your written response, 'including the ability to construct and develop a sustained line of reasoning which is coherent, relevant, substantiated and logically structured' (AQA (2018) GCSE Media Studies, https://filestore.aqa.org.uk/resources/media-studies/AQA-85721-SQP.PDF). In other words, you need to have a clear and logical argument in response to the question, which you back up with references to the CSP(s) named.

Knowledge Check 8.4

Before you continue reading, look at the potential **synoptic question** above, and consider which of the areas of the **theoretical framework**, and which of the contexts you could bring in to your answer:

- **Media Language**
- **Media Representations**
- **Media Audiences**
- **Media Industries**
- **historical**
- **social**
- **cultural**
- **political**.

Knowledge Check 8.5

Look at the following notes for a response to the essay on the following page.

1   Can you identify which areas of the **theoretical framework** each statement refers to?

   Which of the **media contexts** can you see being mentioned?

2   Choose six of the lettered points, and show how each one can be related to the main argument being put forward in the response.

Main argument

Problem for traditional newspapers: Audiences can now access the latest news and entertainment 24 hours a day via the internet, with many websites and apps being free to use. People don't want to get their news just once a day and don't want to pay for it.

Result: print newspapers are losing readers. They are trying to compete, and maintain their audience appeal, by providing something of value in the print edition, and by providing digital and online products themselves.

Could include these points, to tie into the main argument:

a Print newspaper sales falling – *Daily Mirror* sales fell almost 19% in 2017.

b Have to keep the cover price low, to compete with free online products.

c Lower sales means less advertising income for print newspapers.

d Some newspapers have a paywall for their websites. The *Daily Mirror* keeps its online site free to use.

e Initially, websites weren't too much competition, because they could only be accessed from computers – newspapers could be carried around and read anywhere.

f Rise of smartphones has increased the problem, as now digital media is even more portable than newspapers.

g More interactive 1 – stories on the *Daily Mirror* website can be shared via social media, using link icons – helps to market the newspaper.

h More interactive 2 – online readers can contribute to discussions about the articles directly on the webpage – easier than writing letters or emails to a newspaper.

i There is a digital version of the paper (for phone and tablet) – for a subscription fee.

j Demographics of users of *Daily Mirror* print newspaper, digital edition and website.

k *Daily Mirror*'s online advertising is rising, but not as fast as print advertising is falling.

l Buying and printing other newspaper titles has helped to keep print costs down.

m The *Daily Mirror* uses the expected conventions of a newspaper, which are familiar to and appeal to certain parts of the media audience. For example, older people are much more likely to buy newspapers than younger people.

n For some people, reading a newspaper over breakfast or on the way to work is a habit they have always had and will continue with.

o Ageing of print audience could lead to further falls in sales in the future.

p Uses and gratifications theory – people buy newspapers for more than just 'surveillance'. They also value other aspects of the paper, such as puzzles – 'diversion'.

q The *Daily Mirror* represents news stories from a left-wing perspective, which attracts a specific audience, who may not get left-wing news elsewhere.

Publicity still from *Ashes to Ashes*

Use detailed examples

In an extended response question, you may be given a statement and asked how far you agree with it. If so, you can argue the case for or against the statement (or a bit of both). Neither one will be the 'correct answer'. Instead, an important part of your response will be providing evidence for the point of view you are putting forwards.

For example, if one of the television CSPs were *Ashes to Ashes*: Episode 1, in Media Two Section A you could be asked:

Ashes to Ashes was a BBC drama series first broadcast in 2008, following on from the earlier series *Life on Mars*, and was a **hybrid** of police procedural and science fiction **genres**. In the first episode, the main character, Detective Inspector Alex Drake, was shot in 2008 and then woke up in 1981. The series followed her struggle to take part in police activities in 1981, which she saw as key to her regaining consciousness in 2008.

'TV dramas engage an audience's attention through the use of narrative devices.' How far do you agree with this statement? Answer with reference to *Ashes to Ashes*: Episode 1.

A partial response could be:

> The narrative arc in a TV drama often starts with a disruption to the equilibrium and a search to repair the damage caused. Audiences want to know how this will happen, and whether all the characters will come out better in the end. For example, in the first episode of Ashes to Ashes, the main character, DI Alex Drake, is shown apparently being shot in the opening few minutes, so the audience will want to know whether her death can possibly be prevented. They will continue to watch in order to find out. This is also an example of an enigma. Audiences enjoy these because they make people guess ahead, and become actively involved in the story.

Tip ✓

You could use the same question as written for *Ashes to Ashes* to analyse an extract or the full episode of either of your television CSPs. Remember that an extract used in the exam will be about three minutes long.

Use media-specific terminology

As well as being asked short-answer questions that test your understanding of media terminology, you will be expected to use this terminology in each of your answers on both papers. The appropriate use of subject specific terminology is directly assessed, with the expectation that students working at the highest level will be using this terminology effectively throughout their answers.

In Media One, Section A, for example, you could be given a magazine cover such as the one below, to analyse as an unseen source. You should use media terms throughout your answer, making it as detailed and effective as possible.

Knowledge Check 8.6

Read the question and partial response below. How could you improve this response through the use of **media** terminology?

Sample exam question:

Analyse the cover of *Shout* magazine to show how different elements communicate meaning.

A partial response could be:

> The cover has a big picture of The Vamps. It shows them from their feet to the tops of their heads. They are wearing casual clothes and have fashionable hair. As well as the band's name in pink, there is a mint-green shape and white writing over the picture saying 'FUNNY INTERVIEW + FIT POSTERS'. This means people will understand that the words are about them, and that there will be an article about them inside. Three of them are looking at the camera and they are all standing in a casual way. Three are making eye contact with the audience, which suggests that they are friendly and would be happy to get to know the reader. The background is a plain wall, which makes The Vamps stand out. This neutral colour might suggest that they are male, compared with the reader who is probably female.

Shout magazine cover, May 2014

Don't spend too long on the questions you can answer well

Each question will have a limited amount of space for the answer. This should give you plenty of room to respond, if you stick to the relevant information and arguments. The space is intended to give all candidates enough room, including those with large handwriting. If you have small handwriting, you probably won't need all the space you are given. However, as the questions are often open-ended, you may find that you could write far more about some products than will fit into the time.

Use the number of marks to guide you as to how much time you should spend on each question – the more marks given, the longer the proportion of time you should be using. Each exam is 90 minutes long, and carries 84 marks, so if you leave yourself time for checking at the end, one approach could be to use as many minutes as there are marks per question. If you find you are writing for too long on any particular answer, you could move on to ensure you cover the other questions on the paper. In an open-ended analysis response, you wouldn't be expected to write about every single aspect of the product, and if you've been writing for a reasonable length of time you may have already written enough to pick up all the marks you're going to.

You will not be expected to cover a certain number of points in order to get good marks – remember we said there was no set format for answering the questions. Instead, you will gain marks for the *quality* of what you have written, including aspects such as how well you have answered the question that has been set, your level of understanding of the **theoretical framework** and of the contexts of **media**, and your use of **media** terminology.

 Knowledge Check 8.7

Imagine the question about the *Shout* cover on the previous page is worth 12 marks. Time yourself as you write a response to the question. How much can you write in 12 minutes?

Remember to use subject specific terminology and to focus on the intended **meanings** created by the use of **media language**.

Summary

In summary, make sure that you:

- Know and can use subject specific terminology.
- Understand the four areas of the **theoretical framework**: **Media Language**, **Media Representations**, **Media Industries** and **Media Audiences**.
- Understand how **media** contexts have impacted on **media products**.
- Revise thoroughly what you have learned during the course, especially about each of your CSPs.
- Can analyse **media products**, including those you have not seen before.
- Have familiarised yourself with sample or past papers.
- Read the questions carefully.
- Answer the questions that have been set.
- Use your time wisely to ensure you answer all the questions in the right amount of depth.